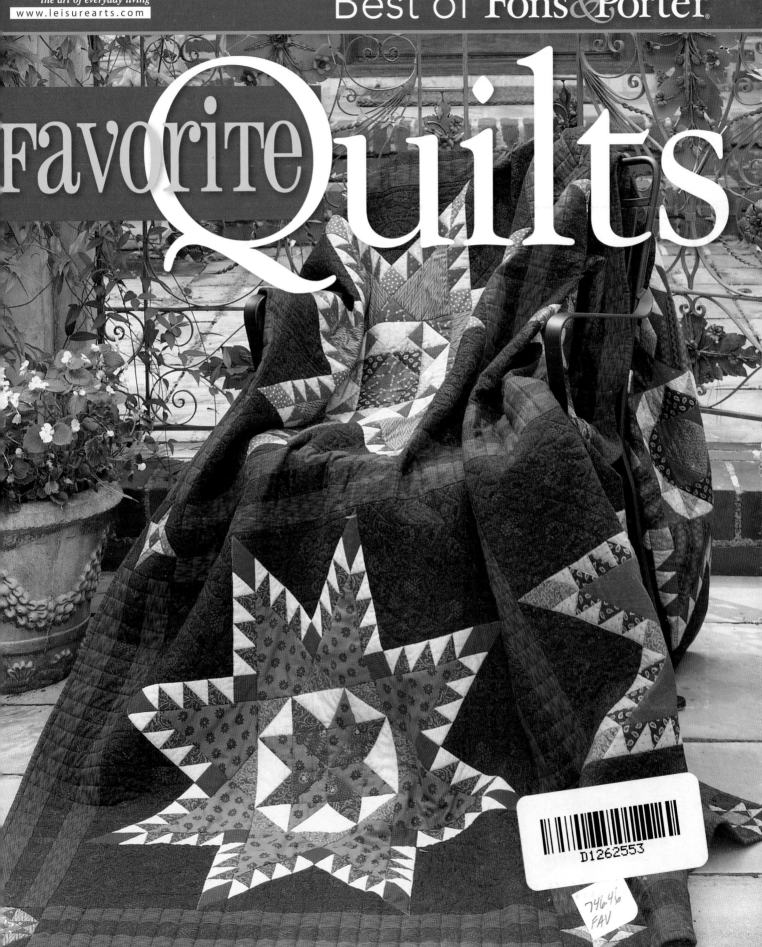

LEISURE ARTS
the art of everyday living
www.leisurearts.com

Best of **Fons&Porter**

Favorite Quilts

FONS & PORTER STAFF
Editors-in-Chief Marianne Fons and Liz Porter

Editor Jean Nolte
Assistant Editor Diane Tomlinson
Managing Editor Debra Finan
Technical Writer Kristine Peterson

Art Director Tony Jacobson

Editorial Assistant Cinde Alexander
Sewing Specialist Cindy Hathaway

Contributing Photographers Craig Anderson, Dean Tanner, Katie Downey
Contributing Photo Assistant DeElda Wittmack

Publisher Kristi Loeffelholz
Advertising Manager Cristy Adamski
Retail Manager Sharon Hart
Web site Manager Phillip Zacharias
Customer Service Manager Tiffiny Bond
Fons & Porter Staff Peggy Garner, Shelle Goodwin, Kimberly Romero, Laura Saner, Karol Skeffington, Yvonne Smith, Natalie Wakeman, Anne Welker, Karla Wesselmann

New Track Media LLC
President and CEO Stephen J. Kent
Chief Financial Officer Mark F. Arnett
President, Book Publishing W. Budge Wallis
Vice President/Publishing Director Joel P. Toner
Vice President, Circulation Nicole McGuire
Vice President, Production Derek W. Corson
Production Manager Dominic M. Taormina
Production Coordinator Kristin N. Burke
IT Manager Denise Donnarumma
New Business Manager Susan Sidler
Renewal and Billing Manager Nekeya Dancy
Online Subscriptions Manager Jodi Lee

Our Mission Statement
Our goal is for you to enjoy making quilts as much as we do.

LEISURE ARTS STAFF
Editor-in-Chief Susan White Sullivan
Quilt and Craft Publications Director Cheryl Johnson
Special Projects Director Susan Frantz Wiles
Senior Prepress Director Mark Hawkins
Imaging Technician Stephanie Johnson
Prepress Technician Janie Marie Wright
Publishing Systems Administrator Becky Riddle
Mac Information Technology Specialist Robert Young

President and Chief Executive Officer Rick Barton
Vice President and Chief Operations Officer Tom Siebenmorgen
Vice President of Sales Mike Behar
Director of Finance and Administration Laticia Mull Dittrich
National Sales Director Martha Adams
Creative Services Chaska Lucas
Information Technology Director Hermine Linz
Controller Francis Caple
Vice President, Operations Jim Dittrich
Retail Customer Service Manager Stan Raynor
Print Production Manager Fred F. Pruss

Library of Congress Control Number: 2011925209
ISBN-13/EAN: 978-1-60900-111-7

We had fun looking through all of the quilts we've made and choosing our favorites to share with you. The projects in this book are some of our most popular of all time. Whether you're looking for a quick and easy project or something more challenging, you're sure to find plenty to love. As you browse through the beautiful photos of the quilts, we think you'll be inspired to start stitching your next project. You'll find quilts in every style—traditional, contemporary, and batik. Our trademarked Sew Easy lessons will guide you via step-by-step photography through any project-specific special techniques. We hope you'll have as much fun making these quilts as we did!

Happy quilting,

Marianne + Liz

Table of Contents

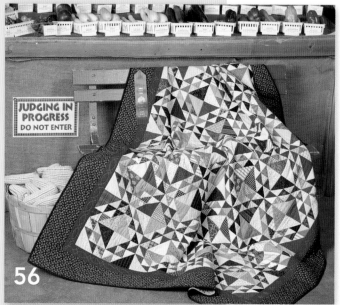

120

130

136

Prairie Stars

Traditionally, the small diamonds for a Prairie Star quilt were individually cut and joined. Quick cutting and piecing methods make short work of assembling the stars for this stunning quilt. Trapunto in the large background squares and rectangles emphasizes the beautiful machine quilting.

PROJECT RATING: CHALLENGING
Size: 91" × 109"
Blocks: 20 (18") Prairie Stars

MATERIALS

7½ yards cream print for
    background, borders, and binding
¼ yard each of 36 assorted prints
    for pieced stars and
    border stars
6 (6") squares assorted prints for
    border stars
¾ yard brown print for vine
8¼ yards backing fabric
King-size quilt batting
Paper-backed fusible web (optional)
Tracing paper
Colored pencils or crayons

- -

Cutting

Measurements include ¼" seam allowances. Follow manufacturer's instructions for using fusible web. Border star pattern is on page 12.

From cream print, cut:

- 1 (2⅝-yard) piece. From this, cut 4 (10"-wide) **lengthwise** strips for borders.
- 4 (11"-wide) strips. From strips, cut 12 (11") C squares.
- 2 (8¾"-wide) strips. From strips, cut 5 (8¾") squares. Cut squares in half diagonally in both directions to make 20 quarter-square B triangles (2 are extra).
- 11 (5¾"-wide) strips. From strips, cut 14 (5¾" × 11") D rectangles and 35 (5¾") A squares.
- 11 (2¼"-wide) strips for binding.

From each ¼-yard piece, cut:

- 1 star for border.
- 5 (1¾"-wide) strips for pieced stars. (Strips need to be at least 24" long for piecing stars.)

From each 6" square, cut:

- 1 star for border.

From brown print, cut:

- 1 (27") square. From this, cut approximately 430" of 1½"-wide continuous bias. Fold bias in thirds, press, and hand baste fold in place to prepare vine.

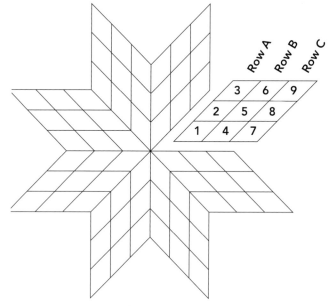

Coloring Diagram

Sample Colored Star Diagram

Star Assembly

1. Trace *Coloring Diagram* onto tracing paper. Determine fabric placement for pieced star and color diagram using colored pencils or crayons. Refer to *Sample Colored Star Diagram* for an example.

2. Join strips for diamonds #1–#3 into a strip set, offsetting strips by approximately 1¾" as shown in *Row A Diagram*. Trim left end of strip set at a 45-degree angle. Place 1¾" mark on ruler atop angled cut. Cut along edge of ruler to make a segment of joined diamonds that is 1¾" wide. Cut 8 Row A segments.

3. In a similar manner, join strips #4–#6 and #7–#9 into strip sets and cut 8 segments from each strip set for Row B and Row C (*Row B Diagram* and *Row C Diagram*).

4. Referring to *Star Point Assembly Diagrams*, lay out 1 each of Row A, B, and C. Join rows to complete 1 star point. Make 8 star points.

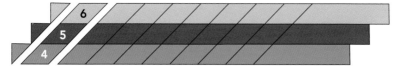

Row A Diagram

Row B Diagram

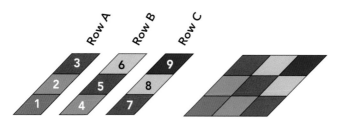

Row C Diagram

Star Point Assembly Diagrams

5. Lay out 8 star points to form a star. Join star points as shown in *Star Assembly Diagram* to make 1 Prairie Star *(Prairie Star Diagram)*. Make 20 Prairie Stars.

Star Assembly Diagram

Prairie Star Diagram

Quilt Assembly

1. Lay out Prairie Stars as shown in photo on page 11.

2. Join 4 Prairie Stars by setting in 1 B triangle at each end of row and 3 A squares between stars as shown in *Star Row Diagram* on page 10. Make 5 star rows.

3. Join rows by setting in 1 D rectangle at each end of row and 3 C squares

Star Row Diagram

Row Joining Diagram

and 4 A squares between stars as shown in *Row Joining Diagram*.

4. Set in D rectangles, A squares, and B triangles around perimeter of quilt to complete quilt center.

Border Assembly

1. Measure quilt length. Cut 2 border strips this length. Add borders to quilt sides. Measure quilt width, including side borders. Cut 2 border strips this length. Add borders to top and bottom edges of quilt.

2. Referring to photo on page 11, position vine and stars along quilt border. Appliqué on borders. Blanket stitch around stars (*Blanket Stitch Diagram*).

Blanket Stitch Diagram

Quilting and Finishing

1. Divide backing fabric into 3 (2¾-yard) pieces. Join pieces lengthwise. Seams will run horizontally.

2. Mark desired quilting designs in background C and D pieces. We used a feathered square design for C squares and half the design for D rectangles.

Refer to *Quilting the Quilt: Fine Feathers* on page 173.

3. If you plan to add trapunto to quilting motifs, refer to *Sew Easy: Trapunto Method for Machine Quilting* on page 13 to baste batting beneath quilting design areas.

4. Layer backing, batting, and quilt top; baste. Quilt as desired. Quilt shown has tiny stipple quilting around trapunto motifs, a ½" grid of squares in A squares and B triangles, and lines spaced ½" apart in border background.

5. Join 2¼"-wide cream print strips into 1 continuous piece for straight-grain French-fold binding. Add binding to quilt.

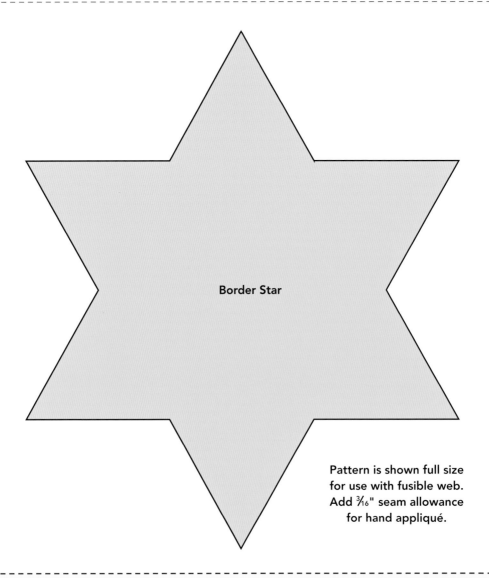

Border Star

Pattern is shown full size
for use with fusible web.
Add ³⁄₁₆" seam allowance
for hand appliqué.

TRIED & TRUE

The photo on page 11 shows some of the many
fabric placement variations that you can try
to give your stars character. Experiment with
the *Coloring Diagram* on page 8 to try some
variations of your own.

Sew Easy™

Trapunto Method for Machine Quilting

Trapunto (or stuffed quilting) emphasizes fancy quilting motifs. We love how it looks for feathered quilting designs since it makes the feather areas puff up. This technique is especially dramatic for whole-cloth quilts and shows up best on solid fabrics.

The basic methods for trapunto when machine quilting are the same for a regular home sewing machine as for a longarm quilting machine.

> If you are working on a garment, cut out outer garment pieces with generous seam allowances to allow for drawing up during quilting and trapunto. Leave garment lining pieces as rectangular shapes so they are easier to layer for quilting.
> —Marilyn

2. Layer marked top fabric and 2 layers of cotton batting. Using water-soluble thread, stitch design *(Photo B)*. Remove from machine.

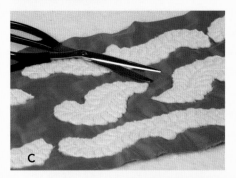

> This is a great way to use all those scraps of batting left from other projects!   —Marilyn

3. Using blunt-tipped scissors, trim batting just outside stitching lines of design areas *(Photo C)*.

4. Layer prepared piece, another layer of cotton batting, and backing fabric. Using thread in color to match top fabric, quilt design *(Photo D)*. Stitching will be atop water-soluble thread.

5. Add additional background quilting around design motifs to help make trapunto areas stand out more *(Photo E)*.

6. Wash piece to remove water-soluble thread.

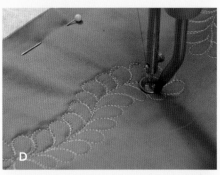

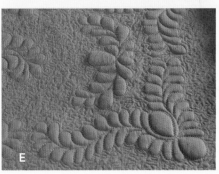

Special Supplies

Chalk marker, Saral® tracing paper, or
  other removable marker
Cotton batting
Water-soluble thread
Colored thread that matches top or
  outer fabric
Blunt-tipped scissors

Instructions

1. Plan placement of quilting motifs *(Photo A)*. Use a chalk marker, Saral® transfer paper, or other removable marker to draw quilting designs onto top layer of fabric.

QUILT BY **Marianne Fons and Liz Porter.**

MACHINE QUILTED BY **Luann Downs**.

One Block Star

Liz and Marianne love "big block" quilts like this one you can cut and sew in an afternoon. It's made of cozy flannel, perfect for wrapping up in on a cold winter day. For a batik version, see Piña Colada on page 19.

PROJECT RATING: EASY

Size: 60" × 72"

MATERIALS

1⅛ yards red small rose print for center star and pieced border

⅞ yard red large rose print for outer star

¾ yard dark green print for middle star and binding

3½ yards beige print for background

4 yards backing fabric

Twin-size quilt batting

15" rotary cutting square (optional)

NOTE: Flannels in the quilt shown are from the Willowberry Winter collection by Willowberry Lane for Maywood Studio.

Cutting

Measurements include ¼" seam allowances.

> ### Sew **Smart**™
> An easy way to cut pieces wider than your standard ruler is to use a 15" ruled square to measure and guide your cuts. —Liz

From red small rose print, cut:

• 5 (6⅞"-wide) strips. From strips, cut 20 (6⅞") squares and 1 (6½") A square. Cut 6⅞" squares in half diagonally to make 40 half-square D triangles.

• 1 (3⅞"-wide) strip. From strip, cut 4 (3⅞") squares. Cut squares in half diagonally to make 8 half-square B triangles.

From red large rose print, cut:

• 2 (12⅞"-wide) strips. From strips, cut 4 (12⅞") squares. Cut squares in half diagonally to make 8 half-square F triangles.

One Block Star

From dark green print, cut:

- 1 (6⅞"-wide) strip. From strip, cut 4 (6⅞") squares. Cut squares in half diagonally to make 8 half-square D triangles.
- 7 (2½"-wide) strips for binding.

From beige print, cut:

- 2 (12⅞"-wide) strips. From strips, cut 4 (12⅞") squares. Cut squares in half diagonally to make 8 half-square F triangles.
- 2 (12½"-wide) strips. From strips, cut 4 (12½") G squares.
- 5 (6⅞"-wide) strips. From strips, cut 24 (6⅞") squares. Cut squares in half diagonally to make 48 half-square D triangles.
- 4 (6½"-wide) strips. From 1 strip, cut 4 (6½") E squares. Piece remaining strips to make 2 (6½" × 48½") H rectangles.
- 1 (3⅞"-wide) strip. From strip, cut 4 (3⅞") squares and 4 (3½") C squares. Cut 3⅞" squares in half diagonally to make 8 half-square B triangles.

Quilt Assembly

1. Join 1 beige print B triangle and 1 red print B triangle to make 1 triangle-square. Make 8 beige/red B triangle-squares.
2. In the same manner, make 8 beige/dark green D triangle-squares, 40 beige/red D triangle-squares, and 8 beige/red F triangle-squares.
3. Lay out red print A square, 8 beige/red B triangle-squares, and 4 beige print C squares as shown in *Center Star Assembly Diagram*. Join into rows; join rows to complete center star *(Center Star Diagram)*.
4. Referring to *Quilt Top Assembly Diagram,* lay out center star, 8 beige/dark green D triangle-squares, and

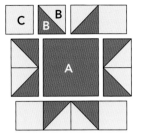

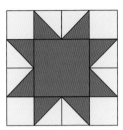

Center Star Assembly Diagram

Center Star Diagram

4 beige print E squares as shown. Join into rows; join rows to complete middle star.

5. Lay out middle star, 8 beige/red F triangle-squares, and 4 beige print G squares as shown. Join into rows; join rows to complete outer star.
6. Add beige print H rectangles to top and bottom of outer star to complete quilt center.
7. Join 8 beige/red D triangle-squares as shown in *Quilt Top Assembly Diagram* to make pieced top border. Repeat to make pieced bottom border. Add borders to quilt center.

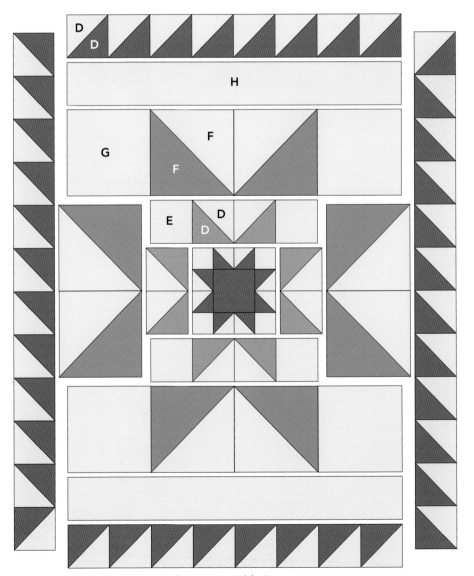

Quilt Top Assembly Diagram

8. Join 12 beige/red D triangle-squares as shown to make 1 pieced side border. Make 2 pieced side borders. Add borders to quilt.

Finishing

1. Divide backing into 2 (2-yard) lengths. Join panels lengthwise. Seam will run horizontally.

2. Layer backing, batting, and quilt top; baste. Quilt as desired. Quilt shown was machine quilted with a feather design in the star points and an allover freehand design in the background *(Quilting Diagram)*.

3. Join 2½"-wide dark green print strips into 1 continuous piece for straight-grain French-fold binding. Add binding to quilt.

Quilting Diagrams

TRIED & TRUE

Use a dark background to set off bright prints. Fabrics shown in this version are from the In an English Garden collection designed by Yolanda Fundora and Barbara Campbell for Lyndhurst Studio. ✳

Piña Colada

This refreshing version of the One Block Star on page 14 uses tropical batiks in juicy colors.

PROJECT RATING: EASY

Size: 60" × 72"

MATERIALS

- 1⅛ yards pink batik for center star and pieced border
- ⅞ yard turquoise batik for outer star
- ¾ yard dark yellow batik for middle star and binding
- 3½ yards light yellow batik for background
- 4 yards backing fabric
- Twin-size quilt batting
- 15" rotary cutting square (optional)

Cutting

From pink batik, cut:

- 5 (6⅞"-wide) strips. From strips, cut 20 (6⅞") squares and 1 (6½") A square. Cut 6⅞"squares in half diagonally to make 40 half-square D triangles.
- 1 (3⅞"-wide) strip. From strip, cut 4 (3⅞") squares. Cut squares in half diagonally to make 8 half-square B triangles.

From turquoise batik, cut:

- 2 (12⅞"-wide) strips. From strips, cut 4 (12⅞") squares. Cut squares in half diagonally to make 8 half-square F triangles.

From dark yellow batik, cut:

- 1 (6⅞"-wide) strip. From strip, cut 4 (6⅞") squares. Cut squares in half diagonally to make 8 half-square D triangles.
- 7 (2¼"-wide) strips for binding.

From light yellow batik, cut:

- 1 (3⅞"-wide) strip. From strip, cut 4 (3⅞") squares and 4 (3½") C squares. Cut 3⅞" squares in half diagonally to make 8 half-square B triangles.
- 5 (6⅞"-wide) strips. From strips, cut 24 (6⅞") squares. Cut squares in half diagonally to make 48 half-square D triangles.
- 4 (6½"-wide) strips. From 1 strip, cut 4 (6½") E squares. Piece remaining strips to make 2 (6½" × 48½") H rectangles.
- 2 (12⅞"-wide) strips. From strips, cut 4 (12⅞") squares. Cut squares in half diagonally to make 8 half-square F triangles.
- 2 (12½"-wide) strips. From strips, cut 4 (12½") G squares.

Quilt Assembly instructions are on page 16.

QUILT BY **Liz Porter.**
MACHINE QUILTED BY **Kelly Ashton**.

Homespun Galaxy

"Plaids are my favorite fabrics. I love collecting them and playing around with them until I find the perfect design," says Liz. This heartwarming quilt is made completely from homespun plaids.

PROJECT RATING: INTERMEDIATE
Size: 71½" × 97"
Blocks: 8 (12") Star blocks
43 (6") Star blocks

MATERIALS

8 fat eighths★ assorted medium/ dark plaids for large star blocks

8 fat quarters★★ assorted medium/ dark plaids for small star blocks

4¼ yards tan plaid for background

3¼ yards red plaid for borders and binding

Fons & Porter Quarter Inch Seam Marker (optional)

6 yards backing fabric

Queen-size quilt batting

★fat eighth = 9" × 20"

★★fat quarter = 18" × 20"

Cutting

Measurements include ¼" seam allowances. Border strips are exact length needed. You may want to make them longer to allow for piecing variations.

From each fat eighth, cut for large stars:
• 1 (5¼"-wide) strip. From strip, cut 2 (5¼") A squares and 1 (4½") B square.

From each fat quarter, cut for small stars:
• 2 (3¼"-wide) strips. From strips, cut 12 (3¼") C squares.
• 1 (2½"-wide) strip. From strip, cut 6 (2½") D squares.

From tan plaid, cut:
• 8 (6½"-wide) strips. From strips, cut 24 (6½" × 12½") E rectangles.
• 3 (5¼"-wide) strips. From strips, cut 16 (5¼") A squares.
• 4 (4½"-wide) strips. From strips, cut 32 (4½") B squares.
• 8 (3¼"-wide) strips. From strips, cut 86 (3¼") C squares.

- 11 (2½"-wide) strips. From strips, cut 172 (2½") D squares.

From red plaid, cut:

- 2 (9¾"-wide) strips. From strips, cut 7 (9¾") squares. Cut squares in half diagonally in both directions to make 28 side setting triangles. (2 are extra.)
- 1 (9⅜"-wide) strip. From strip, cut 2 (9⅜") squares. Cut squares in half diagonally to make 4 half-square corner setting triangles.
- 8 (6½"-wide) strips. Piece strips to make 2 (6½" × 85½") side borders and 2 (6½" × 72") top and bottom borders.
- 9 (2¼"-wide) strips for binding.

Block Assembly

1. Referring to *Sew Easy: Quick Triangle-Squares and Hourglass Units* on page 95, make 8 sets of 4 matching Hourglass Units using 5¼" A squares.

Hourglass Unit Diagrams

2. Referring to *Block Assembly Diagram,* lay out 1 plaid B square, 4 tan B squares, and 4 matching Hourglass Units. Join into rows; join rows to complete 1 large Star block *(Block Diagram).* Make 8 large Star blocks.

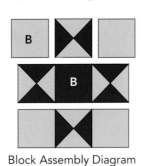

Block Assembly Diagram

Block Diagram

3. Make 172 Hourglass Units using C squares.

4. Referring to *Block Assembly Diagram,* lay out 1 plaid D square, 4 tan D squares, and 4 matching Hourglass Units. Join into rows; join rows to complete 1 small Star block *(Block Diagram).* Make 43 small Star blocks.

Quilt Assembly

1. Referring to *Quilt Top Assembly Diagram,* lay out Star blocks, tan E rectangles, and red plaid setting triangles as shown.

2. Join into diagonal rows; join rows to complete quilt top.

Finishing

1. Divide backing fabric into 2 (3-yard) lengths. Cut 1 piece in half lengthwise to make 2 narrow panels. Join 1 narrow panel to each side of wider panel. Press seam allowances toward narrow panels.

2. Layer backing, batting, and quilt top; baste. Quilt as desired. Quilt shown was quilted with a grid in the star blocks and a feather pattern in the background and borders.

3. Join 2¼"-wide red plaid strips into 1 continuous piece for straight-grain French-fold binding. Add binding to quilt. ✳

Quilting Diagram

TRIED & TRUE

Fussy cut a square from a focus print for the centers of your star blocks. Fabrics shown are from Northcott. ✳

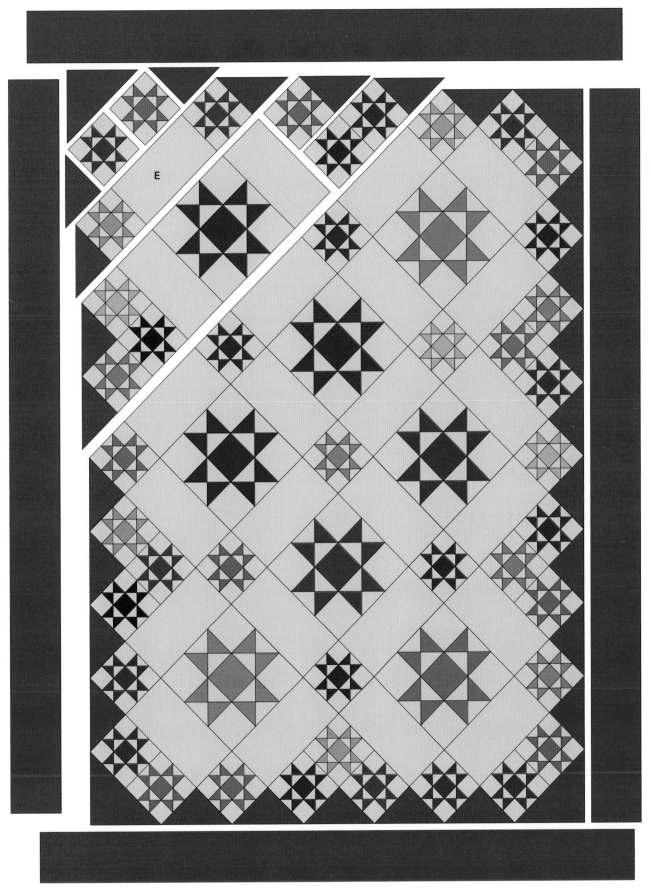

E

Quilt Top Assembly Diagram

Feathered Star

QUILT BY **Liz Porter.**
MACHINE QUILTED BY **Jean Nolte**.

This quilt focuses on the traditional Feathered Star block, with a different smaller star design at the center of each block. The strip sashing has even smaller stars at the intersections. We divided the quilt into sections to simplify the instructions.

PROJECT RATING: ADVANCED

Size: 68¾" × 101"

Blocks: 6 (27⅝") Feathered Star blocks
12 (4½") Sashing blocks

MATERIALS FOR COMPLETE QUILT

⅜ yard each of 6 cream/tan prints

¼ yard red print #1

⅜ yard red print #2

⅝ yard red print #3

⅛ yard red print #4

3½" × 21" strip red print #5

⅜ yard dark gold #1

⅜ yard dark gold #2

¼ yard blue #1

¼ yard blue #2

¼ yard blue #3

3" × 21" strip blue #4

2½"-wide strip blue #5

¼ yard blue stripe

½ yard green #1

3½" × 21" strip green #2

¼ yard green stripe

¼ yard pink print

⅛ yard gold #1

⅓ yard gold #2

⅛ yard brown

⅜ yard black paisley

¼ yard gray stripe

2¾ yards red print #6 for sashing
and binding

4 yards black print for background
and sashing

Template material

6 yards fabric for backing

Twin-size batting

NOTE: Patterns for G and H templates
are on page 46.

Feathered Star Block #1

Scrapbag Star Cutting

From red print #1, cut:

• 2 (2⅝") D squares.

• 8 G.

From dark gold print #1, cut:

• 2 (2⅝") D squares.

From blue print #1, cut:

• 4 (3") squares. Cut squares in half diagonally to make 8 half-square B triangles.

From tan print #1 and black paisley, cut:

• 2 (2⅜"-wide) strips from each. Layer 1 light and 1 dark strip, right sides facing. From strips, cut 24 (2⅜") squares. Cut squares in half diagonally to make 48 pairs of half-square O triangles. Do not separate triangles.

From tan print #1, cut:

• 1 (5½") square. Cut square in half diagonally in both directions to make 4 quarter-square C triangles.

• 2 (3") squares. Cut squares in half diagonally to make 4 half-square B triangles.

• 1 (2⅜"-wide) strip. From strip, cut 8 (2⅜") squares. Cut squares in half diagonally to make 16 half-square O triangles.

From black paisley, cut:

• 1 (4⅜") square. Cut square in half diagonally in both directions to make 4 quarter-square K triangles.

• 2 (3") squares. Cut squares in half diagonally to make 4 half-square B triangles.

From green print #1, cut:

• 8 (2") L squares.

• 8 H.

From black print, cut:

• 1 (12⅝") square. Cut square in half diagonally in both directions to make 4 side triangles.

• 4 (8⁹⁄₁₆") corner squares.

Scrapbag Star Block Assembly

1. Join 2 red print #1 D squares and 2 dark gold print #1 D squares as shown in *Four Patch Unit Diagrams*.

Four Patch Unit Diagrams

2. Join 2 blue print #1 B triangles and 1 tan print #1 C triangle as shown in *Flying Geese Unit Diagrams*. Make 4 Flying Geese Units.

Flying Geese Unit Diagrams

3. Join 1 tan print #1 B triangle and 1 black paisley B triangle as shown in *Triangle-Square Diagrams*. Make 4 triangle-squares.

Triangle Squares Diagrams

4. Lay out Four Patch Unit, Flying Geese Units, and triangle-squares as shown in *Scrapbag Star Block Assembly Diagram*. Join units into rows; join rows to complete block *(Scrapbag Star Block Diagram)*.

Scrapbag Star Block Assembly Diagram

Scrapbag Star Block Diagram

Feathered Star Block Assembly

1. Join pairs of tan print #1 and black paisley O triangles to make 48 triangle-squares.

2. Join 3 triangle-squares and 1 tan print O triangle as shown in *Triangle Unit Diagrams*. Make 8 of each triangle unit as shown.

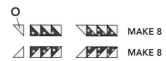

MAKE 8

MAKE 8

Triangle Unit Diagrams

3. Add 1 green print L square to each of 4 triangle units from each group as shown in *Side Feather Unit Diagrams*.

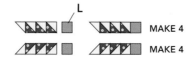

MAKE 4

MAKE 4

Side Feather Unit Diagrams

4. Lay out 2 Side Feather Units and 1 black print side triangle as shown in *Side Triangle Diagrams*. Using partial seams, join feather units to triangle as shown.

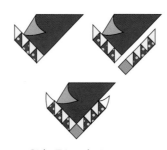

Side Triangle Diagrams

5. Join 2 red print #1 G and 1 black paisley K triangle to side triangle as shown in *Side Unit Diagrams*. Make 4 Side Units.

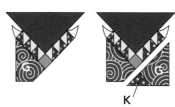

Side Unit Diagrams

6. Add 1 green print #1 H diamond to each remaining feather unit as shown in *Corner Feather Unit Diagrams*. Make 4 of each.

Corner Feather Unit Diagrams

7. Lay out 1 black print corner square and 2 Corner Feather Units as shown in *Corner Unit Diagrams*. Join to complete 1 Corner Unit. Make 4 Corner Units.

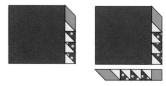

Corner Unit Diagrams

8. Lay out Scrapbag Star block, Side Units, and Corner Units as shown in *Block Assembly Diagram*. Join 1 Side Unit to each side of Star block to make center row.

Block Assembly Diagram

9. Join 2 Corner Units and 1 Side Unit, moving loose side triangles out of the way as shown, to complete top row. Repeat for bottom row.

10. Join rows in the same manner. Finish partial seams to complete Feathered Star block *(Feathered Star Block Diagram)*.

Feathered Star Block Diagram

Feathered Star Block #2

Pinwheel Star Cutting

From red print #2, cut:

• 2 (3") squares. Cut squares in half diagonally to make 4 half-square B triangles.

From dark gold print #1, cut:

• 8 G.

• 4 (3") squares. Cut squares in half diagonally to make 8 half-square B triangles.

From tan print #2 and blue print #1, cut:

• 2 (2⅜"-wide) strips from each. Layer 1 light and 1 dark strip, right sides facing. From strips, cut 24 (2⅜") squares. Cut squares in half diagonally to make 48 pairs of half-square O triangles. Do not separate triangles.

From tan print #2, cut:

• 1 (5½") square. Cut square in half diagonally in both directions to make 4 quarter-square C triangles.

• 2 (3") squares. Cut squares in half diagonally to make 4 half-square B triangles.

• 1 (2⅜"-wide) strip. From strip, cut 8 (2⅜") squares. Cut squares in half diagonally to make 16 half-square O triangles.

From blue print #1, cut:

• 2 (3") squares. Cut squares in half diagonally to make 4 half-square B triangles.

From green print #1, cut:

• 1 (4⅜") square. Cut square in half diagonally in both directions to make 4 quarter-square K triangles.

- 2 (3") squares. Cut squares in half diagonally to make 4 half-square B triangles.

From red print #3, cut:

- 8 (2") L squares.
- 8 H.

From black print, cut:

- 1 (12⅝") square. Cut square in half diagonally in both directions to make 4 side triangles.
- 4 (8⁹⁄₁₆") corner squares.

Pinwheel Star Block Assembly

1. Join 1 red print #2 B triangle and 1 dark gold print #1 B triangle as shown in *Triangle-Square Diagrams*. Make 4 red/gold triangle-squares.

Triangle-Square Diagrams

2. In the same manner, make 4 triangle-squares using 1 green print #1 B triangle and 1 tan print #2 B triangle in each.

3. Join red/gold triangle-squares as shown in *Pinwheel Unit Diagrams*.

Pinwheel Unit Diagrams

4. Join 1 blue print #1 B triangle, 1 dark gold print #1 B triangle, and 1 tan print #2 C triangle as shown in *Flying Geese Unit Diagrams*. Make 4 Flying Geese Units.

Flying Geese Unit Diagrams

5. Lay out Pinwheel Unit, Flying Geese Units, and green/tan triangle-squares as shown in *Pinwheel Star Block Assembly Diagram*. Join units

into rows; join rows to complete block (*Pinwheel Star Block Diagram*).

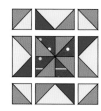

Pinwheel Star Block Assembly Diagram

Pinwheel Star Block Diagram

Feathered Star Block Assembly

1. Join pairs of tan print #2 and blue print #1 O triangles to make 48 triangle-squares.

2. Join 3 triangle-squares and 1 tan print #2 O triangle as shown in *Triangle Unit Diagrams*. Make 8 of each triangle unit as shown.

Triangle Unit Diagrams

3. Add 1 red print #3 square to each of 4 triangle units from each group as shown in *Side Feather Unit Diagrams*.

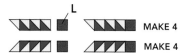

Side Feather Unit Diagrams

4. Lay out 2 Side Feather Units and 1 black print side triangle as shown in *Side Triangle Diagrams*. Using partial seams, join feather units to triangle as shown.

Side Triangle Diagrams

5. Join 2 dark gold print #1 G and 1 green print #1 K triangle to side triangle as shown in *Side Unit Diagrams*. Make 4 Side Units.

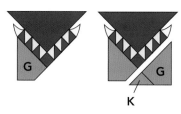

Side Unit Diagrams

6. Add 1 red print #3 H diamond to each remaining feather unit as shown in *Corner Feather Unit Diagrams*. Make 4 of each.

Corner Feather Unit Diagrams

7. Lay out 1 black print corner square and 2 Corner Feather Units as shown in *Corner Unit Diagrams*. Join to complete 1 Corner Unit. Make 4 Corner Units.

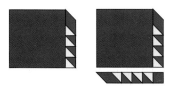

Center Unit Diagrams

8. Lay out Pinwheel Star block, Side Units, and Corner Units as shown in *Block Assembly Diagram*. Join 1 Side

Unit to each side of Star block to make center row.

9. Join 2 Corner Units and 1 Side Unit, moving loose side triangles out of the way as shown, to complete top row. Repeat for bottom row.

Block Assembly Diagram

10. Join rows in the same manner. Finish partial seams to complete Feathered Star block *(Feathered Star Block Diagram)*.

Feather Star Block Diagram

Feathered Star Block #3

Martha Washington's Star Cutting

Measurements include ¼" seam allowances.

From blue print #2, cut:
- 1 (3⅝") square. Cut square in half diagonally in both directions to make 4 quarter-square E triangles.

From green print #2, cut:
- 2 (3") squares. Cut squares in half diagonally to make 4 half-square B triangles.

From red print #3, cut:
- 4 (3") squares. Cut squares in half diagonally to make 8 half-square B triangles.

From tan print #3 and pink print, cut:
- 2 (2⅜"-wide) strips from each. Layer 1 light and 1 dark strip, right sides facing. From strips, cut 24 (2⅜") squares. Cut squares in half diagonally to make 48 pairs of half-square O triangles. Do not separate triangles.

From tan print #3, cut:
- 8 (2⅜"-wide) squares. Cut squares in half diagonally to make 16 half-square O triangles.
- 1 (5½") square. Cut square in half diagonally in both directions to make 4 quarter-square C triangles.
- 2 (3") squares. Cut squares in half diagonally to make 4 half-square B triangles.

From pink print, cut:
- 1 (3⅝") square. Cut square in half diagonally in both directions to make 4 quarter-square E triangles.

From gold print #1, cut:
- 1 (4⅜") square. Cut square in half diagonally in both directions to make 4 quarter-square K triangles.
- 2 (3") squares. Cut squares in half diagonally to make 4 half-square B triangles.

From blue stripe, cut:
- 8 G.

From brown print, cut:
- 8 (2") L squares.
- 8.

From black print, cut :
- 1 (12⅝") square. Cut square in half diagonally in both directions to make 4 side triangles.
- 4 (8⁹⁄₁₆") corner squares.

Martha Washington's Star Block Assembly

1. Join 1 pink print E triangle, 1 blue print #2 E triangle, and 1 green print #2 B triangle as shown in *Corner Unit Diagrams*. Make 4 Corner Units.

Corner Unit Diagrams

2. Join Corner Units to complete Center Unit *(Center Unit Diagram)*.

Center Unit Diagrams

3. Join 2 red print #3 B triangles and 1 tan print #3 C triangle as shown in *Flying Geese Unit Diagrams*. Make 4 Flying Geese Units.

Flying Geese Unit Diagrams

4. Join 1 tan print #3 B triangle and 1 gold print #1 triangle as shown in *Triangle-Square Diagrams*. Make 4 triangle-squares.

Triangle-Square Diagrams

5. Lay out Center Unit, Flying Geese Units, and triangle-squares as shown in *Martha Washington's Star Block Assembly Diagram*. Join into rows; join rows to complete block *(Martha Washington's Star Block Diagram)*.

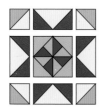

Martha Washington's Star Block Assembly Diagram

Martha Washington's Star Block Diagram

Feathered Star Block Assembly

1. Join pairs of tan print #3 and pink print O triangles to make 48 triangle-squares.

2. Join 3 triangle-squares and 1 tan print #3 O triangle as shown in *Triangle Unit Diagrams*. Make 8 of each triangle unit as shown.

Triangle Unit Diagrams

3. Add 1 brown print L square to each of 4 triangle units from each group as shown in *Side Feather Unit Diagrams*.

Side Feather Unit Diagrams

4. Lay out 2 Side Feather Units and 1 black print side triangle as shown in *Side Triangle Diagrams*. Using partial seams, join feather units to triangle as shown.

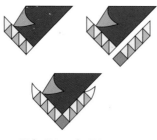

Side Triangle Diagrams

5. Join 2 blue stripe G and 1 gold print #1 K triangle to side triangle as shown in *Side Unit Diagrams*. Make 4 Side Units.

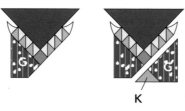

Side Unit Diagrams

6. Add 1 brown print H diamond to each remaining feather unit as shown in *Corner Feather Unit Diagrams*. Make 4 of each.

Corner Feather Unit Diagrams

7. Lay out 1 black print corner square and 2 Corner Feather Units as shown in *Corner Unit Diagrams*. Join to complete 1 Corner Unit. Make 4 Corner Units.

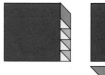

Corner Unit Diagrams

8. Lay out Martha Washington's Star block, Side Units, and Corner Units as shown in *Block Assembly Diagram*. Join 1 Side Unit to each side of Star block to make center row.

Corner Unit Diagrams

9. Join 2 Corner Units and 1 Side Unit, moving loose side triangles out of the way as shown, to complete top row. Repeat for bottom row.

10. Join rows in the same manner. Finish partial seams to complete Feathered Star block *(Feathered Star Block Diagram)*.

Feathered Star Block Diagram

Feathered Star Block #4

Missouri Star Cutting

From blue print #2, cut:

- 1 (4¾") A square.
- 1 (4⅜") square. Cut square in half diagonally in both directions to make 4 quarter-square K triangles.
- 2 (3") squares. Cut squares in half diagonally to make 4 half-square B triangles.

From black paisley print, cut:

- 4 (2⅝") D squares.

From red print #3, cut:

- 2 (3⅜") squares. Cut squares in half diagonally in both directions to make 8 quarter-square F triangles.

From gold print #2, cut:

- 2 (3⅜") squares. Cut squares in half diagonally in both directions to make 8 quarter-square F triangles.

From tan print #4 and red print #4, cut:

- 2 (2⅜"-wide) strips from each. Layer 1 light and 1 dark strip, right sides facing. From strips, cut 24 (2⅜") squares. Cut squares in half diagonally to make 48 pairs of half-square O triangles. Do not separate triangles.

From tan print #4, cut:

- 1 (5½") square. Cut square in half diagonally in both directions to make 4 quarter-square C triangles.

- 2 (3") squares. Cut squares in half diagonally to make 4 half-square B triangles.
- 1 (2⅜"-wide) strip. From strip, cut 8 (2⅜") squares. Cut squares in half diagonally to make 16 half-square O triangles.

From gray stripe, cut:

- 8 G.

From dark gold print #2, cut:

- 8 (2") L squares.
- 8 H.

From black print, cut:

- 1 (12⅝") square. Cut square in half diagonally in both directions to make 4 side triangles.
- 4 (8⁹⁄₁₆") corner squares.

Missouri Star Block Assembly

1. Referring to *Diagonal Seams Diagrams*, place 1 black paisley print D square atop blue print #2 A square, right sides facing. Stitch from corner to corner as shown. Trim ¼" beyond stitching. Press open to reveal triangle. Repeat for remaining corners to complete Center Unit *(Center Unit Diagram)*.

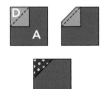

Diagonal Seams Diagrams

Center Unit Diagram

2. Join 1 tan print #4 C triangle, 1 red print #3 F triangle, and 1 gold print #2 F triangle as shown in *Side Unit Diagrams*. Make 4 Side Units.

Side Unit Diagrams

3. Join 1 blue print #2 B triangle and 1 tan print #4 B triangle as shown in *Triangle-Square Diagrams*. Make 4 triangle-squares.

Triangle-Square Diagrams

4. Lay out Center Unit, Side Units, and triangle-squares as shown in *Missouri Star Block Assembly Diagram*. Join units into rows; join rows to complete block *(Missouri Star Block Diagram)*.

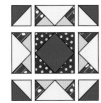

Missouri Star Block Assembly Diagram

Missouri Star Block Diagram

Feathered Star Block Assembly

1. Join pairs of tan print #4 and red print #4 O triangles to make 48 triangle-squares.

2. Join 3 triangle-squares and 1 tan print #4 O triangle as shown in *Triangle Unit Diagrams*. Make 8 of each triangle unit as shown.

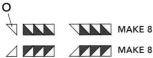

Triangle Unit Diagrams

3. Add 1 dark gold print #2 L square to each of 4 triangle units from each group as shown in *Side Feather Unit Diagrams*.

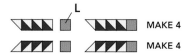

Side Feather Unit Diagrams

4. Lay out 2 Side Feather Units and 1 black print side triangle as shown in *Side Triangle Diagrams*. Using partial seams, join feather units to triangle as shown.

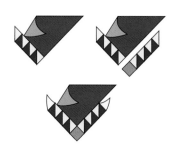

Side Triangle Diagrams

5. Join 2 gray stripe G and 1 blue print #2 K triangle to side triangle as shown in *Side Unit Diagrams*. Make 4 Side Units.

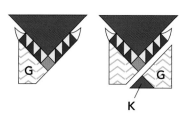

Side Unit Diagrams

6. Add 1 dark gold print #2 H diamond to each remaining feather unit as shown in *Corner Feather Unit Diagrams*. Make 4 of each.

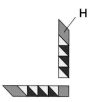

Corner Feather Unit Diagrams

7. Lay out 1 black print corner square and 2 Corner Feather Units as shown in *Corner Unit Diagrams*. Join to complete 1 Corner Unit. Make 4 Corner Units.

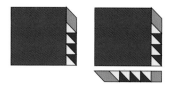

Corner Unit Diagrams

8. Lay out Missouri Star block, Side Units, and Corner Units as shown in *Block Assembly Diagram*. Join 1 Side Unit to each side of Star block to make center row.

Block Assembly Diagram

9. Join 2 Corner Units and 1 Side Unit, moving loose side triangles out of the way as shown, to complete top row. Repeat for bottom row.

10. Join rows in the same manner. Finish partial seams to complete Feathered Star block (*Feathered Star Block Diagram*).

(Diagram N).

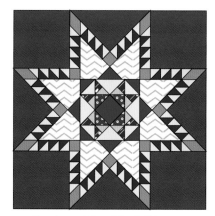

Feathered Star Block Diagram

Feathered Star Block #5

Noon Star Cutting

From green print #1, cut:

- 1 (4¾") A square.

From black paisley print, cut:

- 1 (5½") square. Cut square in in half diagonally in both directions to make 4 quarter-square C triangles.

From tan print #5 and red print #3, cut:

- 2 (2⅜"-wide) strips from each. Layer 1 light and 1 dark strip, right sides facing. From strips, cut 24 (2⅜") squares. Cut squares in half diagonally to make 48 pairs of half-square O triangles. Do not separate triangles.

From tan print #5, cut:

- 2 (3") squares. Cut squares in half diagonally to make 4 half-square B triangles.

- 2 (3⅜") squares. Cut squares in half diagonally in both directions to make 8 quarter-square F triangles.

- 1 (2⅜"-wide) strip. From strip, cut 8 (2⅜") squares. Cut squares in half diagonally to make 16 half-square O triangles.

From red print #3, cut:

- 4 (2⅝") D squares.

From red print #5, cut:

- 1 (4⅜") square. Cut square in half diagonally in both directions to make 4 quarter-square K triangles.

- 2 (3") squares. Cut squares in half diagonally to make 4 half-square B triangles.

From green stripe, cut:

- 8 G.

From gold print #2, cut:

- 2 (3⅜") squares. Cut squares in half in both directions to make 8 quarter-square F triangles.

- 8 (2") L squares.

- 8 H.

From black print, cut:

- 1 (12⅝") square. Cut square in half diagonally in both directions to make 4 side triangles.

- 4 (8⁹⁄₁₆") corner squares.

Noon Star Block Assembly

1. Referring to *Diagonal Seams Diagrams*, place 1 red print #3 D square atop green print #1 A square, right sides facing. Stitch from corner to corner as shown. Trim ¼" beyond stitching. Press open to reveal triangle. Repeat for remaining corners to complete Center Unit (*Center Unit Diagram*).

Diagonal Seams Diagrams

Center Unit Diagram

2. Join 1 black paisley print C triangle, 1 gold print #2 F triangle, and 1 tan print #5 F triangle as shown in *Side Unit Diagrams*. Make 4 Side Units.

Side Unit Diagram

3. Join 1 red print #5 B triangle and 1 tan print #5 B triangle as shown in *Triangle-Square Diagrams*. Make 4 triangle-squares.

Triangle-Square Diagrams

4. Lay out Center Unit, Side Units, and triangle-squares as shown in *Noon Star Block Assembly Diagram*. Join units into rows; join rows to complete block *(Noon Star Block Diagram)*.

Noon Star Block Assembly Diagram

Noon Star Block Diagram

Feathered Star Block Assembly

1. Join pairs of tan print #5 and red print #3 O triangles to make 48 triangle-squares.

2. Join 3 triangle-squares and 1 tan print #5 O triangle as shown in *Triangle Unit Diagrams*. Make 8 of each triangle unit as shown.

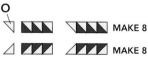

Triangle Unit Diagrams

3. Add 1 gold print #2 L square to each of 4 triangle units from each group as shown in *Side Feather Unit Diagrams*.

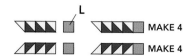

Side Feather Unit Diagrams

4. Lay out 2 Side Feather Units and 1 black print side triangle as shown in *Side Triangle Diagrams*. Using partial seams, join feather units to triangle as shown.

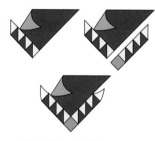

Side Triangle Diagrams

5. Join 2 green stripe G and 1 red print #5 K triangle to side triangle as shown in *Side Unit Diagrams*. Make 4 Side Units.

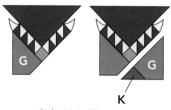

Side Unit Diagrams

6. Add 1 gold print #2 H diamond to each remaining feather unit as shown in *Corner Feather Unit Diagrams*. Make 4 of each.

Corner Unit Diagrams

7. Lay out 1 black print corner square and 2 Corner Feather Units as shown in *Corner Unit Diagrams*. Join to complete 1 Corner Unit. Make 4 Corner Units.

Corner Unit Diagrams

8. Lay out Noon Star block, Side Units, and Corner Units as shown in *Block Assembly Diagram*. Join 1 Side Unit to each side of Star block to make center row.

Block Assembly Diagram

9. Join 2 Corner Units and 1 Side Unit, moving loose side triangles out of the way as shown, to complete top row. Repeat for bottom row.

10. Join rows in the same manner. Finish partial seams to complete Feathered Star block *(Feathered Star Block Diagram)*.

Feathered Star Block Diagram

Feathered Star Block #6

Marianne's Star Cutting

From green print #1, cut:

- 1 (5½") square. Cut square in half diagonally in both directions to make 4 quarter-square H triangles.

From gold print #2, cut:

- 1 (3") square. Cut square in half diagonally to make 2 half-square B triangles.

From pink print, cut:

- 2 (3") squares. Cut squares in half diagonally to make 4 half-square B triangles.

From tan print #6 and dark gold print #2, cut:

- 2 (2⅜"-wide) strips from each. Layer 1 light and 1 dark strip, right sides facing. From strips, cut 24 (2⅜")

squares. Cut squares in half diagonally to make 48 pairs of half-square O triangles. Do not separate triangles.

From tan print #6, cut:

- 1 (2⅜"-wide) strip. From strip, cut 8 (2⅜") squares. Cut squares in half diagonally to make 16 half-square O triangles.
- 2 (3") squares. Cut squares in half diagonally to make 4 half-square B triangles.
- 1 (5½") square. Cut square in half diagonally in both directions to make 4 quarter-square C triangles.

From blue print #1, cut:

- 1 (4⅜") square. Cut square in half diagonally in both directions to make 4 quarter-square K triangles.

- 2 (3") squares. Cut squares in half diagonally to make 4 half-square B triangles.

From red print #2, cut:

- 8 G.
- 1 (3") square. Cut square in half diagonally to make 2 half-square B triangles.

From blue print #3, cut:

- 8 (2") L squares.
- 8 H.

From black print, cut:

- 1 (12⅝") square. Cut square in half diagonally in both directions to make 4 side triangles.
- 4 (8⁹⁄₁₆") corner squares.

Marianne's Star Block Assembly

1. Join 2 gold print #2 B triangles and 2 red print #2 B triangles as shown in *Center Unit Diagrams*.

Center Unit Diagrams

2. Join 1 green print #1 C triangle, and 1 blue print #1 B triangle, 1 tan print #6 B triangle, and 1 pink print B triangle as shown in *Corner Unit Diagrams*. Make 4 Corner Units.

Corner Unit Diagrams

3. Lay out Center Unit, Corner Units, and tan print #6 C triangles as shown in *Marianne's Star Block Assembly Diagram*. Join units into rows; join rows to complete block (*Marianne's Star Block Diagram*).

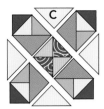

Marianne's Star Block Assembly Diagram

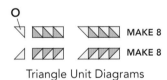

Marianne's Star Block Diagram

Feathered Star Block Assembly

1. Join pairs of tan print #6 and dark gold print #2 O triangles to make 48 triangle-squares.

2. Join 3 triangle-squares and 1 tan print #6 O triangle as shown in *Triangle Unit Diagrams.* Make 8 of each triangle unit as shown.

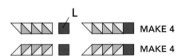

Triangle Unit Diagrams

3. Add 1 blue print #3 L square to each of 4 triangle units from each group as shown in *Side Feather Unit Diagrams.*

Side Feather Unit Diagrams

4. Lay out 2 Side Feather Units and 1 black print side triangle as shown in *Side Triangle Diagrams.* Using partial seams, join feather units to triangle as shown.

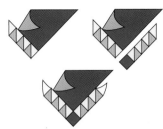

Side Triangle Diagrams

5. Join 2 red print #2 G and 1 blue print #1 K triangle to side triangle as shown in *Side Unit Diagrams.* Make 4 Side Units.

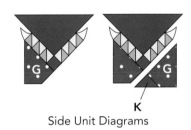

Side Unit Diagrams

6. Add 1 blue print #3 H diamond to each remaining feather unit as shown in *Corner Feather Unit Diagrams.* Make 4 of each.

Corner Feather Unit Diagrams

7. Lay out 1 black print corner square and 2 Corner Feather Units as shown in *Corner Unit Diagrams.* Join to complete 1 Corner Unit. Make 4 Corner Units.

Corner Unit Diagrams

8. Lay out Marianne's Star block, Side Units, and Corner Units as shown in *Block Assembly Diagram.* Join 1 Side Unit to each side of Star block to make center row.

Block Assembly Diagram

9. Join 2 Corner Units and 1 Side Unit, moving loose side triangles out of the way as shown, to complete top row. Repeat for bottom row.

10. Join rows in the same manner. Finish partial seams to complete Feathered Star block *(Feathered Star Block Diagram).*

Feathered Star Block Diagram

Sashing Blocks

Ohio Star Sashing Block Cutting

From gold print #2, cut:
• 4 (2¾") squares. Cut squares in half diagonally in both directions to make 16 quarter-square M triangles.

From blue print #3, cut:
• 2 (2") L squares.

From black print, cut:
• 8 (2") L squares.
• 4 (2¾") squares. Cut squares in half diagonally in both directions to make 16 quarter-square M triangles.

Ohio Star Sashing Block Assembly

1. Join 2 gold print #2 M triangles and 2 black print M triangles as shown in *Hourglass Unit Diagrams*. Make 8 Hourglass Units.

Hourglass Unit Diagrams

2. Lay out 4 Hourglass Units, 4 black print L squares, and 1 blue print L square as shown in *Ohio Star Block Assembly Diagram*. Join into rows; join rows to complete 1 Ohio Star block (*Ohio Star Block Diagram*). Make 2 Ohio Star blocks.

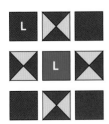

Ohio Star Block Assembly Diagram

Ohio Star Block Diagram

Double Pinwheel Sashing Block Cutting

From red print #3, cut:
• 2 (2") L squares.

From gold print #1, cut:
• 16 (1¼") N squares.

From blue print #3, cut:
• 8 (2") L squares.

From black print, cut:
• 16 (2") L squares.

Double Pinwheel Sashing Block Assembly

1. Referring to *Diagonal Seams Diagrams*, place 1 gold print #1 N square atop red print #3 L square, right sides facing. Stitch from corner to corner as shown. Trim ¼" beyond stitching. Press open to reveal triangle. Repeat for remaining corners to complete Center Unit (*Center Unit Diagram*). Make 2 Center Units.

Diagonal Seams Diagrams

Center Unit Diagram

2. Place 1 blue print #3 L square atop 1 black print L square, right sides facing. Stitch from corner to corner as shown in *Side Unit Diagrams*. Trim ¼" beyond stitching. Press open to reveal triangle. Place 1 gold print #1 N square atop unit; stitch from corner to corner. Trim ¼" beyond stitching. Press open to reveal triangle and complete 1 Side Unit. Make 8 Side Units.

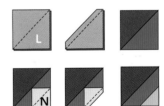

Side Unit Diagrams

3. Lay out 1 Center Unit, 4 Side Units, and 4 black print L squares as shown in *Double Pinwheel Block Assembly Diagram*. Join into rows; join rows to complete block (*Double Pinwheel Block Diagram*). Make 2 Double Pinwheel blocks.

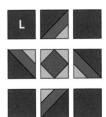

Double Pinwheel Block Assembly Diagram

Double Pinwheel Block Diagram

Gemstone Star Sashing Block Cutting

From red print #3, cut:
- 2 (2") L squares.
- 4 (2¾") squares. Cut squares in half diagonally in both directions to make 16 quarter-square M triangles.

From blue print #4, cut:
- 2 (2¾") squares. Cut squares in half diagonally in both directions to make 8 quarter-square M triangles.
- 8 (1¼") N squares.

From gray stripe, cut:
- 2 (2¾") squares. Cut squares in half diagonally in both directions to make 8 quarter-square M triangles.
- 4 (2⅜") squares. Cut squares in half diagonally to make 8 half-square O triangles.

From black print, cut:
- 4 (2⅜") squares. Cut squares in half diagonally to make 8 half-square O triangles.

Gemstone Star Sashing Block Assembly

1. Referring to *Diagonal Seams Diagrams*, place 1 blue print #4 N square atop 1 red print #3 L square, right sides facing. Stitch from corner to corner as shown. Trim ¼" beyond stitching. Press open to reveal triangle. Repeat for remaining corners to complete Center Unit *(Center Unit Diagram)*. Make 2 Center Units.

Diagonal Seams Diagrams

Center Unit Diagram

2. Join 1 gray stripe M triangle, 2 red print #3 M triangles, and 1 blue print #4 M triangle as shown in *Hourglass Unit Diagrams*. Make 8 Hourglass Units.

Hourglass Unit Diagrams

3. Join 1 gray stripe O triangle and 1 black print O triangle as shown in *Triangle-Square Diagrams*. Make 8 triangle-squares.

Triangle-Square Diagrams

4. Lay out 1 Center Unit, 4 Hourglass Units, and 4 triangle-squares as shown in *Gemstone Star Block Assembly Diagram*. Join into rows; join rows to complete block *(Gemstone Star Block Diagram)*. Make 2 Gemstone Star blocks.

Gemstone Star Block Assembly Diagram

Gemstone Star Block Diagram

Braced Star Sashing Block Cutting

From blue print #5, cut:
- 2 (2") L squares.

From red print #2, cut:
- 4 (2¾") squares. Cut squares in half diagonally in both directions to make 16 quarter-square M triangles.

From green print #2, cut:
- 2 (2¾") squares. Cut squares in half diagonally in both directions to make 8 quarter-square M triangles.

From black print, cut:
- 8 (2") L squares.
- 8 (1¼") N squares.
- 2 (2¾") squares. Cut squares in half diagonally in both directions to make 8 quarter-square M triangles.

Braced Star Sashing Block Assembly

1. Referring to *Diagonal Seams Diagrams*, place 1 black print N square atop 1 blue print #5 L square, right sides facing. Stitch from corner to corner as shown. Trim ¼" beyond stitching. Press open to reveal triangle. Repeat for remaining corners to complete Center Unit *(Center Unit Diagram)*. Make 2 Center Units

Diagonal Seams Diagrams

Center Unit Diagram

2. Join 1 black print M triangle, 1 green print #2 M triangle, and 2 red print #2 M triangles as shown in *Hourglass Unit Diagrams*. Make 8 Hourglass Units.

Hourglass Unit Diagrams

3. Lay out 1 Center Unit, 4 Hourglass Units, and 4 black print L squares as shown in *Braced Star Block Assembly Diagram*. Join into rows; join rows to complete 1 Braced Star block *(Braced*

Star Block Diagram). Make 2 Braced Star blocks.

Braced Star Block Assembly Diagram

Braced Star Block Diagram

Liz's Star Sashing Block Cutting

From red print #2, cut:
- 2 (2") L squares.

From blue print #5, cut:
- 4 (2⅜") squares. Cut squares in half diagonally to make 8 half-square O triangles.

From pink print, cut:
- 2 (2¾") squares. Cut squares in half diagonally in both directions to make 8 quarter-square M triangles.

From green print #1, cut:
- 8 (2") L squares.

From black print, cut:
- 8 (2") L squares.
- 2 (2¾") squares. Cut squares in half diagonally in both directions to make 8 quarter-square M triangles.
- 8 (1¼") N squares.

Liz's Star Sashing Block Assembly

1. Place 1 black print L square atop 1 green print #1 L square, right sides facing. Stitch from corner to corner as shown in *Corner Unit Diagrams.* Trim ¼" beyond stitching. Press

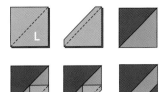

Corner Unit Diagrams

open to reveal triangle. Place 1 black print N square atop unit; stitch from corner to corner. Trim ¼" beyond stitching. Press open to reveal triangle and complete 1 Corner Unit. Make 8 Corner Units.

2. Join 1 blue print #5 O triangle, 1 black print M triangle, and 1 pink print M triangle as shown in *Side Unit Diagrams.* Make 8 Side Units.

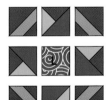

Side Unit Diagrams

3. Lay out 1 red print #2 L square, 4 Corner Units, and 4 Side Units as shown in *Liz's Star Block Assembly Diagram.* Join into rows; join rows to complete 1 Liz's Star block *(Liz's Star Block Diagram).* Make 2 Liz's Star blocks.

Liz's Star Block Assembly Diagram

Liz's Star Block Diagram

Air Castle Sashing Block Cutting

From gold print #1, cut:
- 2 (2") L squares.

From green print #1, cut:
- 4 (2⅜") squares. Cut squares in half diagonally to make 8 half-square O triangles.

From black print, cut:
- 8 (2") L squares.
- 8 (1¼") N squares.
- 2 (2¾") squares. Cut squares in half diagonally in both directions to make 8 quarter-square M triangles.

From red print #3, cut:
- 2 (2¾") squares. Cut squares in half diagonally in both directions to make 8 quarter-square M triangles.

Air Castle Sashing Block Assembly

1. Referring to *Diagonal Seams Diagrams,* place 1 black print N square atop gold print #1 L square, right sides facing. Stitch from corner to corner as shown. Trim ¼" beyond stitching. Press open to reveal triangle. Repeat for remaining corners to complete Center Unit *(Center Unit Diagram).* Make 2 Center Units.

Diagonal Seams Diagrams

Center Unit Diagram

2. Join 1 green print #1 O triangle, 1 black print M triangle, and 1 red print #3 M triangle as shown in *Side Unit Diagrams.* Make 8 Side Units.

Side Unit Diagrams

3. Lay out 1 Center Unit, 4 Side Units, and 4 black print L squares as shown in *Air Castle Block Assembly Diagram*. Join into rows; join rows to complete 1 Air Castle block *(Air Castle Block Diagram)*. Make 2 Air Castle blocks.

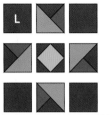

Air Castle Block Assembly Diagram

Air Castle Block Diagram

Quilt Top Assembly

Cutting for Quilt Assembly

From black print, cut:

- 1 (29"-long) piece. From piece, cut 17 (2"-wide) **lengthwise** sashing strips.

From red print #6, cut:

- 2 (29"-long) pieces. From pieces, cut 34 (2"-wide) **lengthwise** sashing strips.
- 9 (2¼"-wide) strips for binding.

Quilt Assembly

1. Referring to *Quilt Top Assembly Diagram,* join 1 black print strip and 2 background strips to make 1 sashing unit. Make 17 sashing units. Measure width of blocks. Trim each sashing unit to that measurement.

2. Lay out Feathered Star blocks, sashing blocks, and sashing units as shown in *Quilt Top Assembly Diagram.*

3. Join into rows; join rows to complete quilt top.

Quilting and Finishing

1. Divide backing fabric into 2 (3-yard) lengths. Cut 1 piece in half lengthwise. Join 1 narrow panel to each side of wider panel. Press seam allowances toward narrow panels.

2. Layer backing, batting, and quilt top; baste. Quilt as desired. Quilt shown was quilted in the ditch and with feather designs and diamond cross-hatching.

3. Join 2¼"-wide red print #6 strips into 1 continuous piece for straight-grain French-fold binding. Add binding to quilt.

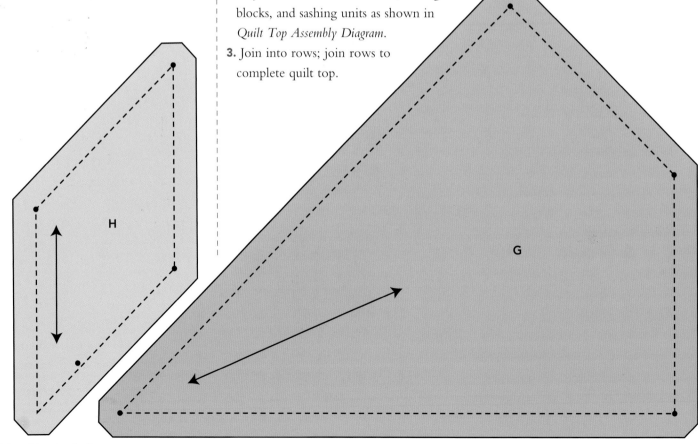

Quilt Top Assembly Diagram

Instead of making just one version of the quilt, we made two! Liz's blocks
all have the same black print background. Marianne's blocks have
a variety of shirting prints for the backgrounds of the stars.

QUILT BY **Liz Porter**.
MACHINE QUILTED BY **Dawn Cavanaugh**.

Pine Burr

"I've always loved this traditional pattern, and decided to make a scrappy version using lots of reproduction prints," says Liz.

PROJECT RATING: CHALLENGING
Size: 65¼" × 83"
Blocks: 12 (17¾") Pine Burr blocks

MATERIALS

⅜ yard each of 12 dark prints for blocks and border corners
½ yard each of 12 light prints for blocks and border corners
2 yards dark blue print for border and binding
Template material
5 yards backing fabric
Twin-size quilt batting

Cutting

Measurements include ¼" seam allowances. Patterns for C, E, F, and G are on page 55. Border strips are exact length needed. You may want to make them longer to allow for piecing variations.

From each dark print, cut:
(Refer to *Dark Fabric Cutting Diagram*.)

• 1 (4") A square.
• 4 C triangles.
• 19 (2⅜") squares. Cut squares in half diagonally to make 38 half-square D triangles.
• 4 E Diamonds.
• 4 F Kite pieces. Mark center of pieces at spot indicated by dot.

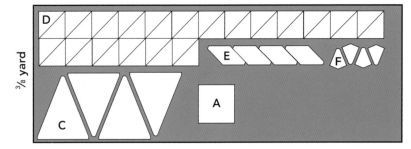

Dark Fabric Cutting Diagram

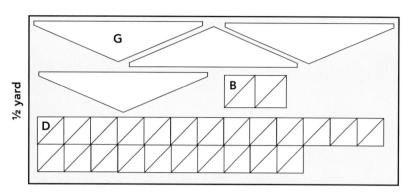

Light Fabric Cutting Diagram

From each light print, cut:

(Refer to *Light Fabric Cutting Diagram*.)

- 2 (3⅜") squares. Cut squares in half diagonally to make 4 half-square B triangles.
- 23 (2⅜") squares. Cut squares in half diagonally to make 46 half-square D triangles.
- 4 G triangles. Mark center of triangles at spot indicated by dot.

From dark blue print, cut:

- 7 (6½"-wide) strips. Piece strips to make 2 (6½" × 71½") top and bottom borders and 2 (6½" × 53¾") side borders.
- 8 (2¼"-wide) strips for binding.

Block Assembly

1. Join 1 dark print A square and 4 light print B triangles as shown in *Center Diagrams.*

Center Diagrams

2. Lay out 10 light print D triangles, 8 dark print D triangles, and 1 dark print F as shown in *Side Triangle Strip Diagrams*. Join pieces to complete

1 Side Triangle Strip. Make 4 Side Triangle Strips.

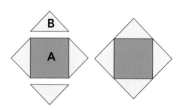

Side Triangle Strip Diagrams

3. Referring to *Block Assembly Diagrams*, join 1 dark print C triangle to each side of center unit.

4. Place 1 Side Triangle Strip atop block center, right sides facing. Pin from one end to center. With triangle strip on top, stitch from outside edge to center dot, pivot, pin other side, and continue stitching to opposite end of block. Repeat for opposite Side Triangle Strip.

5. Join 1 E diamond to each end of remaining 2 Side Triangle Strips. Using same method as in step #4, join triangle strips to remaining sides of block.

6. Place 1 G triangle atop block, right sides facing. Pin layers from end to center, matching center of G triangle with center of block. With G triangle on top, stitch from outside edge to center dot, pivot, pin other side, and continue stitching to opposite end of

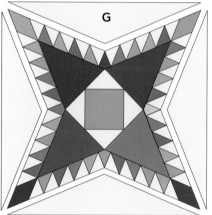

Block Assembly Diagrams

Block Diagram

triangle. Repeat for remaining sides to complete 1 Pine Burr block (*Block Diagram*). Make 12 blocks.

Quilt Assembly

1. Lay out blocks as shown in *Quilt Top Assembly Diagram*. Join into rows; join rows to complete quilt center.

Quilt Top Assembly Diagram

2. Add side borders to quilt center.

3. Join 1 light print D triangle and 1 dark print D triangle to make a triangle-square. Make 64 triangle-squares. Lay out 16 triangle-squares as shown in *Border Corner Diagram*. Join into

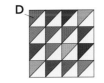

Border Corner Diagram

rows; join rows to complete 1 Border Corner. Make 4 Border Corners.

4. Join 1 Border Corner to each end of top and bottom borders. Add borders to quilt.

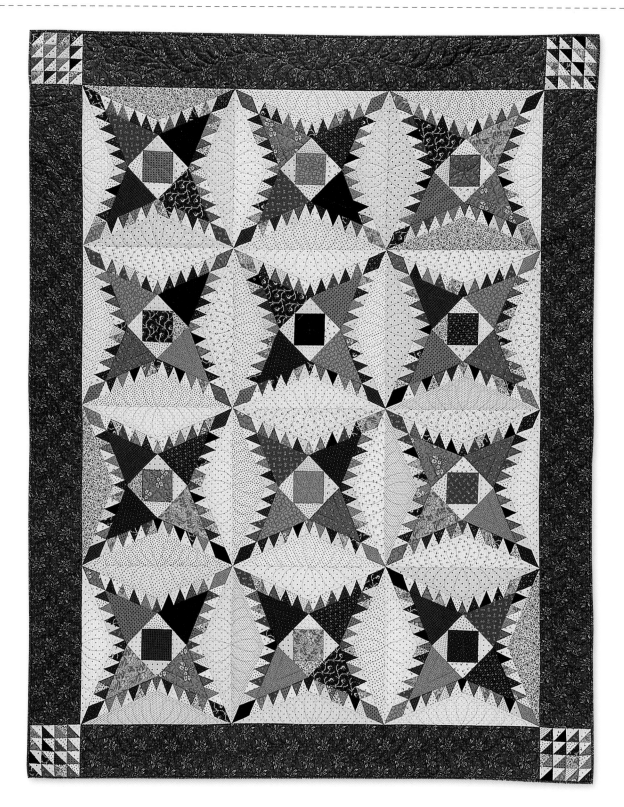

Finishing

1. Divide backing into 2 (2½-yard) pieces. Cut 1 piece in half lengthwise to make 2 narrow panels. Join 1 narrow panel to each side of wider panel; press seam allowances toward narrow panels.

2. Layer backing, batting, and quilt top; baste. Quilt as desired. Quilt shown was quilted in the ditch around blocks, Side Triangle Strips, and Border Corners, and has feather designs in the light background areas and borders.

3. Join 2¼"-wide dark blue print strips into 1 continuous piece for straight-grain French-fold binding. Add binding to quilt. ✳

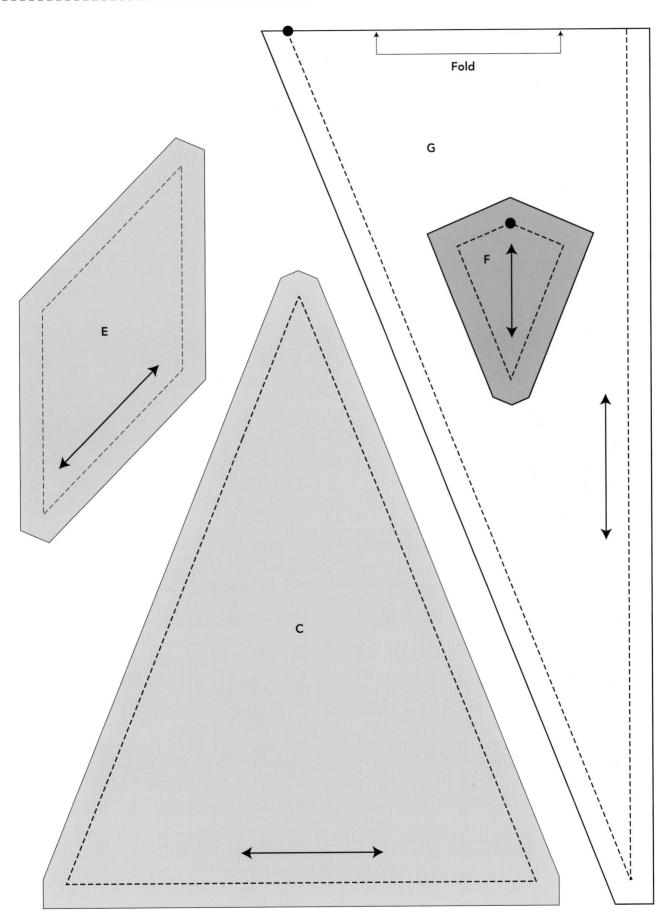

Fold

G

F

E

C

Corn and Beans

On display in the horticultural building at the Iowa State Fair are rows of fruits and vegetables proudly produced in family gardens. Judges award blue ribbons to the best pumpkins, tomatoes, cucumbers, and relishes. The traditional Corn and Beans pattern, made here from hundreds of scraps, reflects the variety and abundance of food in rural America.

PROJECT RATING: INTERMEDIATE
Size: 62" × 86"
Blocks: 24 (12") Corn and Beans blocks

MATERIALS

12 fat quarters★ assorted medium/dark prints (Use more fabrics for a scrappier look.)

12 fat quarters★ assorted light prints

⅝ yard red print for inner border

1½ yards brown print for outer border

⅝ yard black print for binding

5¼ yards backing fabric

Twin-size quilt batting

★fat quarter = 18" × 20"

Cutting

Measurements include ¼" seam allowances. Border strips are exact length needed. You may want to make them longer to allow for piecing variations.

From each fat quarter, cut:

- 1 (4⅞"-wide) strip. From strip, cut 4 (4⅞") squares. Cut squares in half diagonally to make 8 half-square B triangles.
- 4 (2⅞"-wide) strips. From strips, cut 20 (2⅞") squares. Cut squares in half diagonally to make 40 half-square A triangles.

From red print, cut:

- 7 (2½"-wide) strips. Piece strips to make 2 (2½" × 72½") side inner borders and 2 (2½" × 52½") top and bottom inner borders.

From brown print, cut:

- 8 (5½"-wide) strips. Piece strips to make 2 (5½" × 76½") side outer borders and 2 (5½" × 62½") top and bottom outer borders.

From black print, cut:

- 8 (2¼"-wide) strips for binding.

Block Assembly

1. Lay out 5 light A triangles, 5 medium/dark A triangles, 1 light B triangle and 1 medium/dark B triangle as shown in *Quadrant Diagrams*. Join pieces to complete 1 quadrant. Make 4 quadrants.

Quadrant Diagrams

2. Lay out 4 quadrants as shown in *Block Assembly Diagram*. Join into rows; join rows to complete 1 Corn and Beans block *(Block Diagram)*. Make 24 blocks.

Block Assembly Diagram

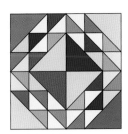

Block Diagram

Quilt Assembly

1. Lay out blocks as shown in *Quilt Top Assembly Diagram.*

2. Join blocks into rows; join rows to complete quilt center.

3. Add red print side inner borders to quilt center. Add red print top and bottom inner borders to quilt.

4. Repeat for brown print outer borders.

Finishing

1. Divide backing fabric into 2 (2⅝-yard) lengths. Cut 1 piece in half lengthwise to make 2 narrow panels. Join 1 narrow panel to each side of wider panel. Press seam allowances toward narrow panels.

2. Layer backing, batting, and quilt top; baste. Quilt as desired. Quilt shown was quilted in the ditch in the blocks, with an egg-and-dart pattern in the inner border, and a vine in the outer border.

3. Join 2¼"-wide black print strips into 1 continuous piece for straight-grain French-fold binding. Add binding to quilt.

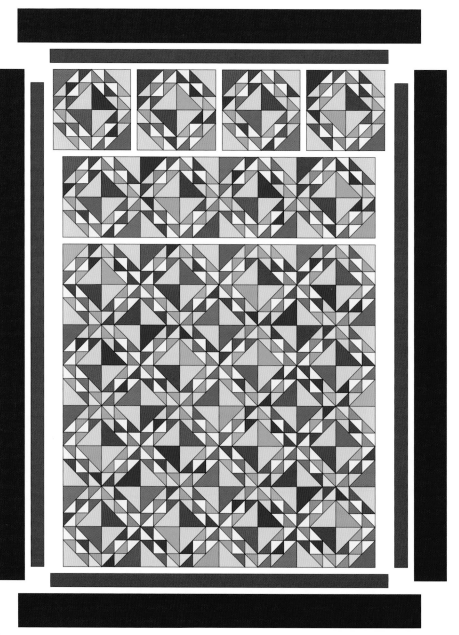

Quilt Top Assembly Diagram

TRIED & TRUE

Bright, cheery 1930s prints combined with muslin are featured in the blocks in our wallhanging. The yellow and green borders are the colors of corn and beans.

QUILT BY **Marianne Fons**.
MACHINE QUILTED BY **Jean Nolte**.

Marianne's Star Chain

Marianne made this quilt in both traditional circa 1900 colors and in contemporary colors that are popular today. "I made a quilt that looks turn-of-the-century" she says.

PROJECT RATING: INTERMEDIATE
Size: 63" × 78"
Blocks: 20 (14") Star Chain Blocks

MATERIALS

1½ yards white print for blocks
2¼ yards gray print for blocks, sashing, border, and binding
1½ yards pink print for blocks
1¼ yards navy print for blocks
1 yard black-and-white stripe for blocks
1 yard red print for blocks
¾ yard blue print for blocks
5 yards fabric for backing
Twin-size batting

Cutting
Measurements include ¼" seam allowances.

From white print, cut:
- 2 (2½"-wide) strips. From strips, cut, 20 (2½") A squares.
- 30 (1½"-wide) strips. From 8 strips, cut 194 (1½") B squares. Remaining strips are for strip sets.

From gray print, cut:
- 2 (14½"-wide) strips. From strips, cut 49 (1½" × 14½") sashing strips.
- 18 (1½"-wide) strips. From 17 strips, cut 18 (1½" × 12½") border strips, 80 (1½" × 2½") C rectangles, and 164 (1½") B squares. Remaining strip is for border strip set.
- 8 (2¼"-wide) strips for binding.

From pink print, cut:
- 4 (12½"-wide) strips. From 2 strips, cut 40 (1½" × 12½") rectangles. Remaining strips are for strip sets.

From navy print, cut:
- 4 (10½"-wide) strips. From 2 strips, cut 40 (1½" × 10½") rectangles. Remaining strips are for strip sets.

From black-and-white stripe, cut:
- 4 (8½"-wide) strips. From 2 strips, cut 40 (1½" × 8½") rectangles. Remaining strips are for strip sets.

From red print, cut:
- 4 (6½"-wide) strips. From 2 strips, cut 40 (1½" × 6½") rectangles. Remaining strips are for strip sets.

From blue print, cut:
- 4 (4½"-wide) strips. From 2 strips, cut 40 (1½" × 4½") rectangles. Remaining strips are for strip sets.

Block Assembly

1. Referring to *Center Unit Diagrams*, place 1 gray print B square atop 1 white print A square, right sides facing. Stitch diagonally from corner to corner. Trim ¼" beyond stitching. Press open to reveal triangle. Repeat for remaining corners to complete Center Unit.

Center Unit Diagrams

2. Referring to *Side Unit Diagrams*, place 1 white print B square atop 1 gray print C rectangle, right sides facing Stitch diagonally from corner to corner as shown. Trim ¼" beyond stitching. Press open to reveal triangle. Repeat for opposite end of rectangle to complete 1 Side Unit. Make 4 Side Units.

Side Unit Diagrams

3. Referring to *Star Assembly Diagrams*, lay out center unit, 4 side units, and 4 gray print B squares. Join into rows; join rows to complete 1 Star block center. Make 20 Star block centers.

Star Assembly Diagrams

4. Join 2 white print strips and 1 blue print strip as shown in *Strip Set Diagram*. Make 2 strip sets. From strip sets, cut 40 (1½"-wide) segments.

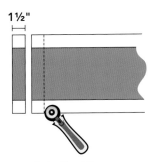

1½"

Strip Set Diagram

5. In a similar manner, make 2 strip sets each using white print strips and red print, black-and-white stripe, navy print, and pink print center strips. From strip sets, cut 40 (1½"-wide) segments of each color combination.

6. Referring to *Block Assembly Diagrams*, join 1 Star block center, 2 blue print rectangles, and 2 blue/white segments as shown.

7. In the same manner, referring to *Block Assembly Diagrams*, join red print, black-and-white stripe, navy, print and pink print rectangles and strip set segments to center to complete 1 Star Chain block (*Block Diagram*).

8. Make 20 Star Chain blocks.

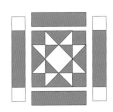
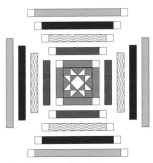

Block Assembly Diagrams

Block Diagram

Quilt Assembly

1. Referring to *Pre-Sashing Diagrams*, pre-sash blocks using gray print sashing strips and white print B squares.

2. Lay out pre-sashed blocks as shown in *Quilt Top Assembly Diagram*. Join blocks into rows; join rows to complete quilt center.

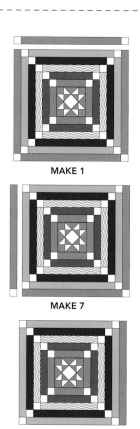

MAKE 1

MAKE 7

MAKE 12

Pre-Sashing Diagrams

3. Join 2 white print strips and 1 gray print strip as shown in *Strip Set Diagram*. From strip set, cut 18 (1½"-wide) segments.

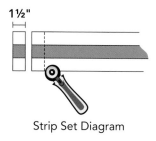

1½"

Strip Set Diagram

4. Referring to *Quilt Top Assembly Diagram*, join 4 segments, 5 gray print border strips, 2 white print B squares, and 2 gray print B squares to make 1 pieced side border. Make 2 pieced side borders. Add borders to quilt center.

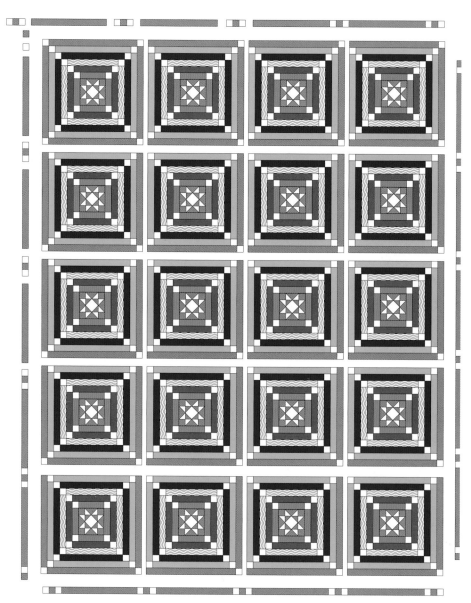

Quilt Top Assembly Diagram

5. Join 5 segments and 4 gray print border strips to make pieced top border. Repeat for pieced bottom border. Add borders to quilt.

Quilting and Finishing

1. Divide backing fabric into 2 (2½-yard) lengths. Cut 1 piece in half lengthwise. Join 1 narrow panel to each side of wider panel. Press seam allowances toward narrow panels.

2. Layer backing, batting, and quilt top; baste. Quilt as desired. Quilt shown was quilted in the ditch in center star area and with feather motifs in the strip area around stars.

3. Join 2¼"-wide gray print strips into 1 continuous piece for straight-grain French-fold binding. Add binding to quilt. ✳

Washington Pavement

Liz likes to work in reproduction fabrics, and also likes to choose patterns that a quiltmaker from the past might have used. Album-style blocks like *Washington Pavement* were favorites among Civil War era quiltmakers.

PROJECT RATING: INTERMEDIATE
Size: 57½" × 79½"
Blocks:
35 (8½") Washington Pavement blocks

MATERIALS

Note: Liz used more fabrics than listed here for a scrappier look.

18 fat eighths★ assorted medium/
   dark prints for blocks
2¼ yards tan for block background
2½ yards dark brown print for
   sashing and binding
½ yard gold print for sashing
   squares
5 yards backing fabric
Twin-size quilt batting
★fat eighth = 9" × 20"

Cutting

Measurements include ¼" seam allowances.

From each fat eighth, cut:
• 4 (2"-wide) strips. From strips, cut
   2 (2" × 13") rectangles for strip sets,
   8 (2" × 5") B rectangles, and
   6 (2") A squares.

From tan print, cut:
• 38 (2"-wide) strips. From strips, cut
   70 (2" × 13") rectangles for strip sets,
   and 280 (2") A squares.

From dark brown print, cut:
• 7 (9"-wide) strips. From strips, cut
   82 (9" × 3") sashing strips.
• 8 (2¼"-wide) strips for binding.

From gold print, cut:
• 4 (3"-wide) strips. From strips, cut
   48 (3") sashing squares.

Block Assembly

1. Join 2 (2" × 13") tan rectangles and 1 (2" × 13") medium/dark rectangle as shown in *Strip Set Diagram*. Make 35 strip sets. From each strip set, cut 6 (2"-wide) segments.

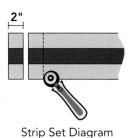

Strip Set Diagram

2. Choose 1 set of 6 matching strip set segments and 2 A squares from 1 medium/dark print, 4 matching B rectangles and 1 A square from another medium/dark print, and 8 tan A squares as shown in *Block Assembly Diagrams*. Join pieces as shown.

Block Assembly Diagrams

3. Trim block ¼" beyond corners of squares as indicated by dotted lines in *Trimming Diagram* to complete 1 Washington Pavement block *(Block Diagram)*. Make 35 blocks.

Trimming Diagram

Block Diagram

Quilt Assembly

1. Lay out blocks, sashing strips, and sashing squares as shown in photo on page 67.

2. Join into rows; join rows to complete quilt top.

Finishing

1. Divide backing fabric into 2 (2½-yard) pieces. Cut 1 piece in half lengthwise to make 2 narrow panels. Join 1 narrow panel to each side of wider panel; press seam allowances toward narrow panels.

2. Layer backing, batting, and quilt top; baste. Quilt as desired. Quilt shown was quilted with concentric squares in the blocks and straight lines in the sashing.

3. Join 2¼"-wide dark brown print strips into 1 continuous piece for straight-grain French-fold binding. Add binding to quilt.

TRIED & TRUE

For contemporary contrast, try using bright prints such as these from the "Daisy May" collection by P & B Textiles.

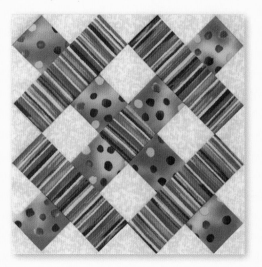

QUILT BY **Liz Porter.**
MACHINE QUILTED BY **Jean Nolte.**

Gentleman's Fancy

Make this quilt for your guy to wrap up in when he watches his favorite ball games on TV.

PROJECT RATING: INTERMEDIATE

Size: 58½" × 85½"

Blocks: 6 (22½") Gentleman's Fancy blocks

MATERIALS

Note: Liz used plaid and check flannels for her quilt. You can give your quilt an entirely different look by choosing geometric or floral print fabrics.

6 fat quarters★ assorted black plaids for blocks

6 fat quarters★ assorted red plaids for blocks

½ yard each of 6 tan plaids for block backgrounds

1⅛ yards tan plaid for sashing

2½ yards red check for sashing and binding

5¼ yards backing fabric

Twin-size quilt batting

★fat quarter = 18" × 20"

Cutting

Measurements include ¼" seam allowances.

From each of 3 red and 3 black fat quarters, cut:

- 2 (5⅜"-wide) strips. From strips, cut 6 (5⅜") squares. Cut squares in half diagonally to make 12 half-square A triangles.
- 1 (5") B square.

From each of remaining 3 red and 3 black fat quarters, cut:

- 5 (2"-wide) strips for strip sets.

From each tan plaid 1/2-yard piece, cut:

- 1 (5⅜"-wide) strip. From strip, cut 6 (5⅜") squares. Cut squares in half diagonally to make 12 half-square A triangles.
- 1 (5"-wide) strip. From strip, cut 4 (5") B squares.
- 2 (2"-wide) strips. Cut strips in half to make 4 (2" × 20") strips for strip sets.

From 1⅛ yards tan plaid, cut:

- 5 (2"-wide) strips for strip sets.
- 1 (23"-wide) strip. From strip, cut 17 (23" × 2") strips for sashing.

From red check, cut:

- 4 (2"-wide) strips for strip sets.
- 2 (23"-wide) strips. From strips, cut 34 (23" × 2") strips for sashing.
- 8 (2½"-wide) strips for binding.

> ## Sew **Smart**™
> When making flannel quilts, I like to cut my binding strips 2½" wide. —Liz

Block Assembly

1. Join 1 red and 1 tan A triangle as shown in *Triangle-Square Diagrams*. Make 12 matching triangle-squares.

Triangle-Square Diagrams

2. Join 1 tan and 2 black 2"-wide strips as shown in *Dark Strip Set Diagram*. Make 2 strip sets. From dark strip sets, cut 4 (2"-wide) segments and 4 (5"-wide) segments.

Dark Strip Set Diagram

3. Join 1 black and 2 tan 2"-wide strips as shown in *Light Strip Set Diagram*. From strip set, cut 8 (2"-wide) segments.

Light Strip Set Diagram

4. Join 2 light and 1 dark (2"-wide) strip set segments to make 1 Nine Patch Unit *(Nine Patch Unit Diagrams)*. Make 4 Nine Patch Units.

Nine Patch Unit Diagrams

5. Lay out 4 Nine Patch Units, 4 (5"-wide) dark segments, 12 triangle-squares, 4 tan B squares, and 1 red B square as shown in *Block Assembly Diagram*. Join into rows; join rows to complete 1 red Gentleman's Fancy block *(Red Block Diagram)*. Make 3 red blocks.

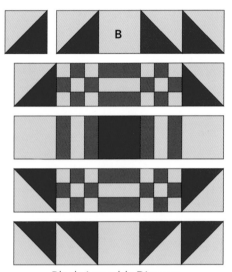

Block Assembly Diagram

Red Block Diagram

7. In a similar manner, make 3 black Gentleman's Fancy blocks *(Black Block Diagram)*.

Black Block Diagram

Sashing Assembly

1. Join 2 (2" × 23") red check strips and 1 (2" × 23") tan plaid strip to make 1 sashing unit. Make 17 sashing units.

2. Join 2 (2"-wide) red check strips and 1 (2"-wide) tan plaid strip to make 1 dark strip set. From strip set, cut 12 (2"-wide) dark segments.

3. Join 2 (2"-wide) tan plaid strips and 1 (2"-wide) red check strip to make 1 light strip set. Make 2 light strip sets. From strip sets, cut 24 (2"-wide) light segments.

4. Join 2 light segments and 1 dark segment to make Nine Patch sashing square (*Nine Patch Unit Diagrams*). Make 12 Nine Patch sashing squares.

Quilt Assembly

1. Lay out blocks, sashing units, and Nine Patch sashing squares as shown in *Quilt Top Assembly Diagram* on page 72 and photograph on page 73.

2. Join into rows; join rows to complete quilt top.

Finishing

1. Divide backing fabric into 2 (2⅝-yard) pieces. Cut 1 piece in half lengthwise to make 2 narrow panels. Join 1 narrow panel to each side of wider panel. Press seam allowances toward narrow panels.

2. Layer quilt top, batting, and backing; baste. Quilt as desired. Quilt shown was quilted in the ditch in the sashing and nine patch units and with circles in the blocks (*Quilting Diagram*).

3. Join 2½"-wide red check binding strips into 1 continuous piece for straight-grain French-fold binding. Add binding to quilt.

Quilting Diagram

TRIED & TRUE

Perky giraffes peer out from the center of this African-themed version of the Gentleman's Fancy block. All fabrics are from Timeless Treasures.

Quilt Top Assembly Diagram

QUILT BY **Liz Porter.**

MACHINE QUILTED BY **Kelly Ashton.**

Rodeo

A chenille lasso loops around the edge of Liz's easy flannel *Rodeo* quilt. Plaid strip sets are stitched in a Rail Fence pattern, and machine quilted western motifs graze along the border.

PROJECT RATING: EASY

Size: 66" × 90"

MATERIALS

18 fat quarters★ assorted flannel prints for strip sets

3 yards burgundy flannel for border and binding

⅝ yard tan plaid flannel for lasso appliqué on border

5½ yards backing fabric

Temporary spray adhesive

Full-size quilt batting

★fat quarter = 18" × 20"

Cutting

Measurements include ¼" seam allowances. Border strips are exact length needed. You may want to make them longer to allow for piecing variations.

From each fat quarter, cut:

• 11 (1½"-wide) strips.

From burgundy flannel, cut:

• 8 (9½"-wide) strips. Piece strips to make 2 (9½" × 72½") side borders and 2 (9½" × 66½") top and bottom borders.

• 9 (2½"-wide) strips for binding.

> **Sew Smart™**
>
> When making flannel quilts, I like to cut my binding strips 2½" wide. —Liz

From tan plaid flannel, cut:

• 2 (20") squares. Cut squares in half diagonally to make 4 half-square triangles. Join 2 triangles as shown in *Bias Strip Cutting Diagrams* on page 76. Repeat for remaining triangles. Layer 2 joined triangles, spraying lightly with temporary spray adhesive to hold layers together. Cut approximately 600" of ½"-wide two-layer bias strips from layered pieced units.

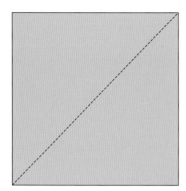

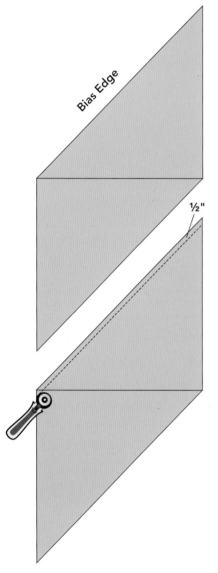

Bias Strip Cutting Diagrams

Quilt Assembly

1. Join 6 (1½"-wide) print strips as shown in *Strip Set Diagram*. Make 32 strip sets.

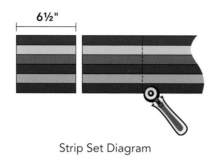

6½"

Strip Set Diagram

2. From each strip set, cut 3 (6½"-wide) segments.

3. Lay out segments as shown in photo on page 77. Join segments into rows; join rows to complete quilt center.

4. Add side borders to quilt center. Add top and bottom borders to quilt.

5. Referring to photo on page 77, use a pencil or chalk to lightly mark placement line for lasso on border. Center layered bias strips on drawn line and pin in place. Add additional layered strips to cover entire line, butting ends together. Stitch along center of bias strips.

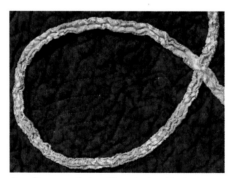

A soft rope of chenille stitched in loops around the border corrals *Rodeo*'s strip-pieced blocks, giving this quilt a Wild West playfulness.

Quilting and Finishing

1. Divide backing fabric into 2 (2¾-yard) lengths. Cut 1 piece in half lengthwise to make 2 narrow panels. Join 1 narrow panel to each side of wider panel. Press seam allowances toward narrow panels.

2. Layer backing, batting, and quilt top; baste. Quilt as desired. Quilt shown was quilted with western motifs surrounded by an allover meandering pattern.

3. Join 2½"-wide burgundy print strips into 1 continuous piece for straight-grain French-fold binding. Add binding to quilt.

4. Wash and dry quilt to fray the edges of the lasso appliqué.

TRIED & TRUE

The soft floral fabrics in this version are from the "Whispers in the Wind" collection by Moda.

Texas Log Cabin

Marianne combined a variety of 1890s-style reproduction prints for her classic Log Cabin quilt. She arranged the blocks in a Sunshine and Shadow setting and appliquéd stars where the light shirting prints come together. Marianne explains, "I grew up in Texas, and the star shape I used on the blocks and in the border reminds me of a Texas Ranger's badge."

PROJECT RATING: INTERMEDIATE
Size: 67" × 94"
Blocks: 96 (6¾") Log Cabin blocks

MATERIALS

38 fat quarters★ assorted dark prints in red, blue, grey, green, pink, purple, brown, and gold
20 fat quarters★ assorted light prints in beige, tan, and cream
1 yard red solid for block centers, inner border, and binding
5¾ yards backing fabric
Paper-backed fusible web
Full-size quilt batting
★fat quarter = 18" × 20"

Cutting

Measurements include ¼" seam allowances. Because there are so many pieces which are similar in size, you may want to label them as you cut. Border strips are exact length needed. You may want to make them longer to allow for piecing variations. Patterns for Stars are on page 84. Follow manufacturer's instructions for using fusible web.

From dark print fat quarters, cut a total of:

- 304 (1¼"-wide) strips. From strips, cut:
  - 96 each strips #15 and #16
  - 142 strip #12
  - 164 each strips #11, #8, #7, #4, and #3
  - 8 strip #1
- 24 Large Stars.
- 30 Small Stars.

See *Cutting Chart for 1 Log Cabin Block* for strip lengths.

From light print fat quarters, cut a total of:

- 240 (1¼"-wide) strips. From strips, cut:
  - 96 strip #14
  - 126 strip #13
  - 156 each strips #10, #9, #6, #5, and #2
  - 134 strip #1

See *Cutting Chart for 1 Log Cabin Block* for strip lengths.

From red solid, cut:

- 9 (2¼"-wide) strips for binding.
- 4 (1¼"-wide) strips. From strips, cut 126 (1¼") center squares.
- 7 (⅞"-wide) strips. Piece strips to make 2 (⅞" × 81½") side inner borders and 2 (⅞" × 55¼") top and bottom inner borders.

Cutting Chart for 1 Log Cabin Block
CUT ALL STRIPS 1¼" WIDE

Dark Strips	Light Strips	Strip Length
#16		7¼"
#15	#14	6½"
#12	#13	5¾"
#11	#10	5"
#8	#9	4¼"
#7	#6	3½"
#4	#5	2¾"
#3	#2	2"
	#1	1¼"

Log Cabin Block Assembly

1. Lay out pieces as shown in *Log Cabin Block Diagram*.

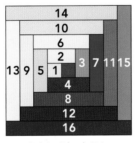

Log Cabin Block Diagram

2. Join strips in numerical order to complete 1 Log Cabin block. Make 96 Log Cabin blocks.

3. Join 4 Log Cabin blocks to make 1 Block Unit *(Block Unit Diagram)*. Referring to *Quilt Top Assembly Diagram* for placement, appliqué 1 Large Star to center of Block Unit.

Sew Smart™

To avoid stiffness when appliquéing stars, window the fusible web and cut away background fabric from behind stars. See *Sew Easy: Windowing Fusible Appliqué* on page 85. —Marianne

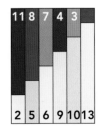

Block Unit Diagram

Quilt Assembly

1. Lay out Block Units as shown in *Quilt Top Assembly Diagram*. Join into horizontal rows; join rows to complete quilt center.

2. Add red side inner borders to quilt center. Add top and bottom inner borders to quilt.

Log Cabin Border Assembly

1. Lay out dark and light pieces as shown in *Border Unit A Diagram*. Join strip #2 to strip #11, strip #5 to strip #8, strip #6 to strip #7, strip #9 to strip #4, strip #10 to strip #3, and strip #13 to red center. Join strips to make 1 Border Unit A. Make 30 Border Unit A. In the same manner, make 30 Border Unit B *(Border Unit B Diagram)*.

Border Unit A Diagram

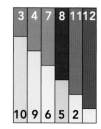

Border Unit B Diagram

2. Join 1 Border Unit A and 1 Border Unit B. Appliqué 1 Small Star over seam between units. Make 30 A/B Border Units.

3. Join 1 dark strip #12 and one light square #1 to make 1 Border Unit C *(Border Unit C Diagram)*. Make 8 Border Unit C.

Border Unit C Diagram

4. Lay out strips as shown in *Corner Block Diagrams*. Join pieces in numerical order to make 1 Corner block. Make 4 Corner blocks.

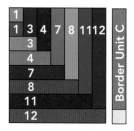

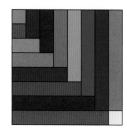

Corner Block Diagrams

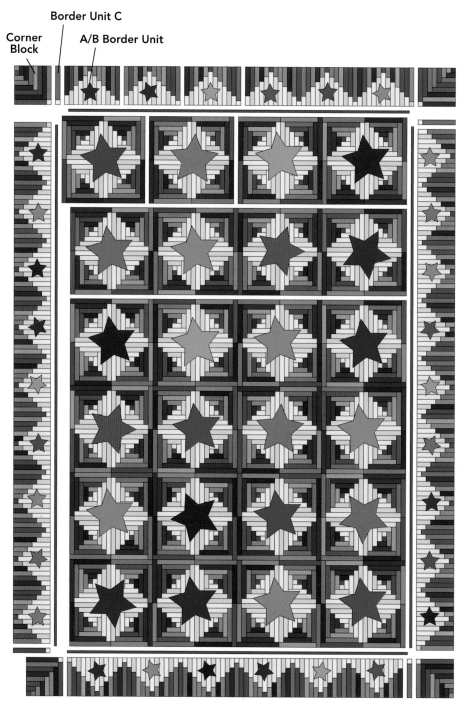

Quilt Top Assembly Diagram

5. Add one Border Unit C to each Corner Block as shown in *Corner Block Diagrams*.

6. Referring to *Quilt Top Assembly Diagram*, lay out 9 appliquéd border units and 1 Border Unit C as shown. Join to make side border. Repeat for opposite side border. Add borders to quilt.

7. Lay out 6 appliquéd border units, 1 Border Unit C, and 2 Corner blocks as shown. Join to make top border. Repeat for bottom border. Add borders to quilt.

Finishing

1. Divide backing into 2 (2⅞-yard) pieces. Cut 1 piece in half lengthwise to make 2 narrow panels. Join 1 narrow panel to each side of wider panel; press seam allowances toward narrow panels.

2. Layer backing, batting, and quilt top; baste. Quilt as desired. Quilt shown is outline quilted around stars and has star motifs in large stars, diamonds in light areas, and concentric circles in dark areas *(Quilting Diagram)*.

3. Join 2¼"-wide red strips into 1 continuous piece for straight-grain French-fold binding. Add binding to quilt.

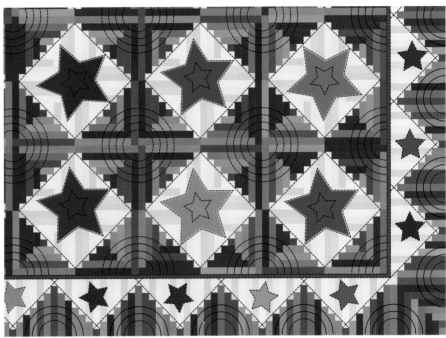

Quilting Diagram

Texas Log Cabin Table Runner

MATERIALS

6 fat eighths★ assorted dark prints
6 fat eighths★ assorted light prints
6" square red solid
½ yard border fabric
⅜ yard binding fabric
1⅛ yards backing fabric
24" × 45" piece quilt batting
★fat eighth = 9" × 20"

Cutting

NOTE: Refer to *Cutting Chart for 1 Log Cabin Block* on page 80 to cut pieces for blocks.

From each of 3 dark prints, cut:
• 1 Large Star.
• 2 sets of dark strips.

From each of remaining 3 dark prints, cut:
• 2 sets of dark strips.

From each light print, cut:
• 2 sets of light strips.

From red solid, cut:
• 12 (1¼") center squares.

From border fabric, cut:
• 4 (3½"-wide) strips. Piece strips to make 2 (3½" × 41") top and bottom borders and 2 (3½" × 20") side borders.

From binding fabric, cut:
• 4 (2¼"-wide) strips. ✳

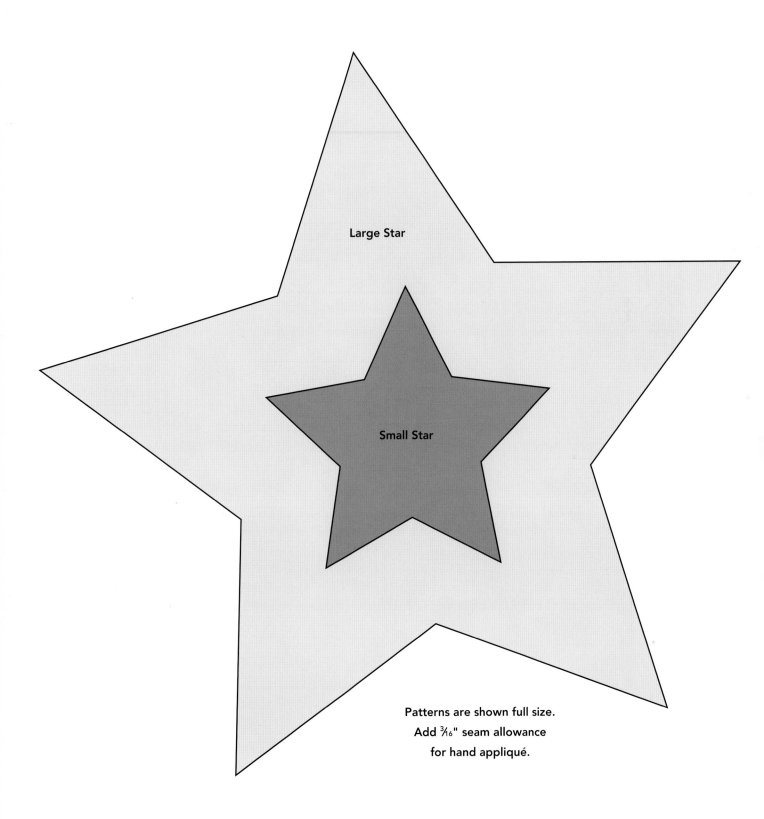

Large Star

Small Star

Patterns are shown full size.
Add ³⁄₁₆" seam allowance
for hand appliqué.

Windowing Fusible Appliqué

Try our method for utilizing fusible web that keeps appliqués
soft and flexible. It's perfect for *Texas Log Cabin*.

Choose a lightweight "sewable" fusible product. The staff at your favorite quilt shop can recommend brands. Always read and follow manufacturer's instructions for proper fusing time and iron temperature.

Sew **Smart**™

Fused shapes will be the reverse of the pattern you trace. If it's important for an object to face a certain direction, make a reverse pattern to trace. We do this quickly by tracing the design on tracing paper, then turning the paper over and tracing the design through onto the other side of the paper. —Marianne

1. Trace appliqué motifs onto paper side of fusible web, making a separate tracing for each appliqué needed *(Photo A)*.
2. Roughly cut out drawn appliqué shapes, cutting about ¼" outside drawn lines *(Photo B)*.
3. "Window" the fusible by trimming out the interior of the shape, leaving a scant ¼" inside drawn line *(Photo C)*.

Follow manufacturer's instructions to fuse web side of each shape to wrong side of appliqué fabric.

4. Cut out appliqués, cutting carefully on drawn outline *(Photo D)*. Only a thin band of fusible web frames the shape.
5. Peel off paper backing *(Photo E)*. Position appliqué in place on background fabric, and follow manufacturer's instructions to fuse shapes in place.

Sew **Smart**™

If you have trouble peeling off the paper backing, try scoring paper with a pin to give you an edge to begin with. —Liz

B

C

D

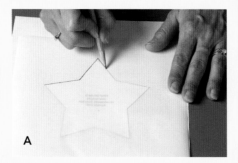

A

E

QUILT BY **Marianne Fons**.
MACHINE QUILTED BY **Dawn Cavanaugh**.

Our Home Sweet Home

Marianne created this spectacular medallion quilt. She says, "This is the largest quilt I've ever made. It was a labor of love for the king-size bed in our newly-remodeled bedroom. The house represents our own—white with a black roof and two red chimneys."

PROJECT RATING: CHALLENGING
Size: 108" × 108"

MATERIALS

- 1 fat eighth★ each white, gold, blue, red, and 2 black-and-white prints for house, roof, and sky
- 1 fat quarter★★ each of 32 assorted medium/dark red, blue, gold, green, and black prints
- ¾ yard large red floral print for center medallion and border corners
- 3½ yards cream print for center medallion background, star blocks, and borders
- 3¼ yards blue stripe for sashing
- 3½ yards tan floral print for star borders and triangle border
- Paper-backed fusible web
- ⅞ yard red dot for binding
- Fons & Porter Half & Quarter Ruler (optional)
- Fons & Porter Quarter Inch Seam Marker (optional)
- Fons & Porter Easy Diagonal Sets Ruler (optional)
- EZ Tri-Recs™ Tri Tool (optional)
- 9¾ yards backing fabric
- King-size quilt batting
- ★fat eighth = 9" × 20"
- ★★fat quarter = 18" × 20"

Cutting

Measurements include ¼" seam allowances. Patterns for appliqué shapes and P triangle are on page 93. Because there are so many pieces which are similar in size, you may want to label them as you cut. Border strips are exact length needed. You may want to make them longer to allow for piecing variations. If you are using the Fons & Porter Half & Quarter Ruler to cut J and K triangles for star points, refer to *Sew Easy: Making Flying Geese Units* on page 94. If you are using the Tri-Recs™ Tri Tool to cut P triangles for triangle border, refer to *Sew Easy: Using Tri-Recs Tool* on page 97.

From white print fat eighth, cut:
• 4 (2½" × 6½") C rectangles.
• 3 (2½") A squares.

From gold print fat eighth, cut:
• 1 (2½") A square.

From blue print fat eighth, cut:
• 1 (1½" × 12½") E rectangle.
• 2 (4") squares for foundation piecing roof sections #3 and #4.
• 2 (2½" × 3½") D rectangles.
• 1 (2½") A square.

From red print fat eighth, cut:
• 2 (2½") A squares.

From black-and-white print #1, cut:
• 1 (4" × 8") rectangle for foundation piecing roof section #2.

From black-and-white print #2, cut:
• 1 (4" × 9½") rectangle for foundation piecing roof section #1.
• 1 (2½" × 4½") B rectangle.

From assorted medium/dark print fat quarters, cut a total of:
• 4 matching Leaves.
• 4 matching Leaves reversed.
• 4 matching Flowers.
• 4 matching Centers.
• 5 (4½"-wide) strips. From strips, cut 64 P triangles.

• 36 (4¼") squares for Hourglass Units.
  NOTE: If not using the Fons & Porter Quarter Inch Seam Marker to make Houglass units, cut squares in half diagonally in both directions to make 144 quarter-square J triangles.
• 50 (3⅞") squares. Cut squares in half diagonally to make 100 half-square R triangles.
• 16 (3") squares. Cut squares in half diagonally to make 32 half-square G triangles.
• 256 (2⅜") squares, cutting multiples of 4 from each fabric. Cut squares in half diagonally to make 512 half-square K triangles.
• 256 (2") L squares, cutting multiples of 2 from each fabric.

From large red floral print, cut:
• 1 (9⅜"-wide) strip. From strip, cut 2 (9⅜") squares. Cut squares in half diagonally to make 4 half-square F triangles.
• 1 (4½"-wide) strip. From strip, cut 4 (4½") Q squares.
• 1 (3½"-wide) strip. From strip, cut 12 (3½") O squares.
• 1 (2⅝"-wide) strip. From strip, cut 4 (2⅝") H squares.
• 1 (2½"-wide) strip. From strip, cut 12 (2½") A squares.
• 1 (2"-wide) strip. From strip, cut 8 (2") L squares.

From cream print, cut:
• 1 (15⅞"-wide) strip. From strip, cut 2 (15⅞") squares. Cut squares in half diagonally to make 4 half-square I triangles.

Refer to Sew Easy: Making Flying Geese Units on page 94 to cut quarter-square J triangles for Star blocks using the Fons & Porter Half & Quarter Ruler.
• 16 (2"-wide) strips. From strips, cut 256 quarter-square J triangles.

NOTE: If not using the Fons & Porter Half & Quarter Ruler, cut: 8 (4¼"-wide) strips. From strips, cut 64 (4¼") squares. Cut squares in half diagonally in both directions to make 256 quarter-square J triangles for Star blocks.
• 4 (4¼"-wide) strips. From strips, cut 36 (4¼") squares for Hourglass Units.
  NOTE: If not using the Fons & Porter Quarter Inch Seam Marker to make Hourglass Units, cut squares in half diagonally in both directions to make 144 quarter-square J triangles **or** cut 9 (2"-wide) strips. From strips, cut 144 quarter-square J triangles using the Fons & Porter Half & Quarter Ruler.
• 5 (3⅞"-wide) strips. From strips, cut 50 (3⅞") squares. Cut squares in half diagonally to make 100 half-square R triangles.
• 2 (3"-wide) strips. From strips, cut 16 (3") squares. Cut squares in half diagonally to make 32 half-square G triangles.
• 13 (2"-wide) strips. From strips, cut 256 (2") L squares.

From blue stripe, cut:
• 11 (3½"-wide) strips. Piece strips to make 4 (3½" × 102½") sashing #6.
• 18 (2½"-wide) strips. Piece strips to make 4 (2½" × 81½") sashing strip #5, 4 (2½" × 60½") sashing strip #3, and 4 (2½" × 30½") sashing strip #1.
• 13 (2"-wide) strips. Piece strips to make 4 (2" × 72½") sashing strip #4 and 4 (2" × 51½") sashing strip #2.

From tan floral print, cut:
Refer to Sew Easy: Cutting Setting Triangles on page 96 to cut M and N triangles using the Fons & Porter Easy Diagonal Sets Ruler.
• 20 (4¾"-wide) strips. From strips, cut 120 M setting triangles and 16 half-square N setting triangles.

NOTE: If not using the Fons & Porter Easy Diagonal Sets Ruler, cut:

- 8 (9¾"-wide) strips. From strips, cut 30 (9¾") squares. Cut squares in half diagonally in both directions to make 120 M setting triangles.
- 2 (5⅛"-wide) strips. From strips, cut 8 (5⅛") squares. Cut squares in half diagonally to make 16 half-square N setting triangles.
- 5 (4½"-wide) strips. From strips, cut 68 P triangles.

From red dot, cut:

- 12 (2¼"-wide) strips for binding.

Center House Roof Assembly

1. Draw a 3" × 12" rectangle on tracing paper or other lightweight paper.
2. Referring to *Roof Unit Foundation Piecing Diagram*, measure and draw lines as shown. (Pattern is reversed for paper foundation piecing.) Add ¼" seam allowances around large rectangle.

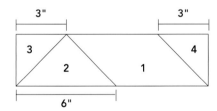

Roof Unit Foundation Piecing Diagram

3. Foundation piece roof section in numerical order.
4. Trim roof unit to 3½" × 12½", trimming on outer drawn lines of paper pattern. Remove paper.

House Assembly

1. Referring to *House Assembly Diagram*, lay out pieces as shown.
2. Join into sections; join sections to complete House Unit.

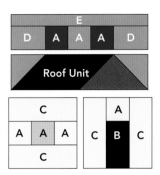

House Assembly Diagram

Center Medallion Assembly

1. Join red floral print half-square F triangles to House Unit.
2. Join 1 cream print G triangle and 1 medium/dark print G triangle to make 1 triangle-square. Make 32 triangle-squares.
3. Lay out triangle-squares and red floral print H squares as shown in *Center Medallion Assembly Diagram*.
4. Join 8 triangle-squares; add to 1 side of quilt center. Repeat for opposite side.

5. Join 8 triangle-squares and 2 red floral print H squares as shown in *Center Medallion Assembly Diagram*. Add to top of quilt center. Repeat for bottom of quilt.
6. Join cream print I triangles to quilt center.
7. Referring to photo on page 87, appliqué flowers and leaves on cream print triangles.
8. Referring to *Center Medallion Assembly Diagram*, join 1 blue stripe sashing strip #1 to left side of quilt center. Repeat for opposite side. Join 1 red floral print A square to each end of 2 remaining sashing strip #1. Add strips to top and bottom of quilt.

Star Block Assembly

1. Referring to *Star Block Assembly Diagram* on page 90, use 8 matching medium/dark K triangles and 4 cream print J triangles to make 4 Flying Geese Units. Make 64 sets of 4 matching Flying Geese Units.

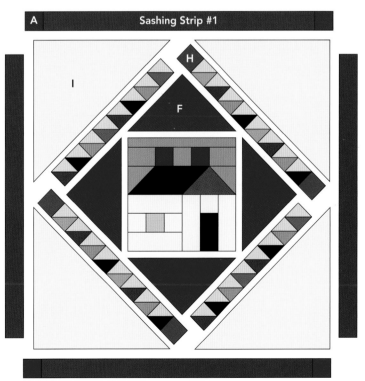

Center Medallion Assembly Diagram

2. Lay out 4 matching Flying Geese Units, 2 pairs of medium/dark L squares, and 4 cream print L squares as shown. Join into rows; join rows to complete 1 Star block *(Star Block Diagram).* Make 64 Star blocks.

Star Block
Assembly Diagram

Star Block Diagram

Inner Star Border Assembly

1. Lay out 4 Star blocks, 6 tan floral print M triangles, and 2 tan floral print N triangles as shown in *Quilt Top Assembly Diagram* on page 91. Join pieces to make top inner star border. Add border to top of quilt center. Repeat for bottom inner star border.

2. Lay out 4 Star Blocks and 8 tan floral print M triangles as shown in *Quilt Top Assembly Diagram.* Join pieces to make side inner star border. Add border to quilt center. Repeat for opposite side inner star border.

3. Join 1 Star block, 2 tan floral print M triangles, and 1 tan floral print N triangle to make border corner. Add to quilt center. Repeat for remaining 3 corners.

4. Referring to *Quilt Top Assembly Diagram,* join 1 blue stripe sashing strip #2 to left side of quilt center. Repeat for opposite side. Join 1 red floral print L square to each end of 2 remaining sashing strip #2. Add strips to top and bottom of quilt.

Hourglass Border

1. Refer to *Sew Easy: Quick Triangle-Squares and Hourglass Units* on page 95 to make 72 Hourglass Units using medium/dark print 4¼" squares and cream print 4¼" squares. **NOTE:** If not using the Fons & Porter Quarter Inch Seam Marker, join 2 matching J triangles and 2 cream print J triangles to make 1 Hourglass Unit *(Hourglass Unit Diagrams).* Make 72 Hourglass Units.

Hourglass Unit Diagrams

2. Referring to *Quilt Top Assembly Diagram,* join 18 Hourglass Units, alternating directions, to make 1 Hourglass Border. Make 4 Hourglass Borders. Add 1 Hourglass Border to left side of quilt center. Repeat for opposite side. Add 1 red floral print O square to each end of remaining 2 Hourglass Borders; add borders to top and bottom of quilt.

3. Referring to *Quilt Top Assembly Diagram,* join 1 blue stripe sashing strip #3 to left side of quilt center. Repeat for opposite side. Add 1 red floral print A square to each end of 2 remaining sashing strip #3. Add strips to top and bottom of quilt.

Triangle Border

1. Lay out 16 medium/dark P triangles and 17 tan floral P triangles as shown in *Quilt Top Assembly Diagram.* Join triangles to make 1 Triangle Border. Square off ends of border as shown. Make 4 borders.

2. Add 1 triangle border to left side of quilt. Repeat for opposite side.

3. Add 1 red floral print Q square to each end of remaining 2 Triangle Borders.

Add borders to top and bottom of quilt.

4. Join 1 blue stripe sashing strip #4 to left side of quilt center. Repeat for opposite side. Join 1 red floral print L square to each end of 2 remaining sashing strip #4. Add strips to top and bottom of quilt.

Sawtooth Border

1. Join 1 cream print R triangle and 1 medium/dark print R triangle to make a triangle-square. Make 100 triangle-squares.

2. Join 25 triangle-squares to make 1 Sawtooth Border *(Quilt Top Assembly Diagram).* Make 4 Sawtooth Borders. Add 1 Sawtooth Border to left side of quilt top. Repeat for opposite side.

3. Add 1 red floral print O square to each end of remaining 2 Sawtooth Borders. Add borders to top and bottom of quilt.

4. Join 1 blue stripe sashing strip #5 to left side of quilt center. Repeat for opposite side. Join 1 red floral print A square to each end of 2 remaining sashing strip #5. Add strips to top and bottom of quilt.

Outer Star Border Assembly

1. Lay out 10 Star blocks, 18 tan floral print M triangles, and 2 tan floral print N triangles as shown in *Quilt Top Assembly Diagram.* Join pieces to make top outer Star Border. Add border to top of quilt. Repeat for bottom Star Border.

2. Lay out 10 Star blocks and 20 tan floral print M triangles as shown in *Quilt Top Assembly Diagram.* Join pieces to make side outer Star Border. Add border to left side of quilt. Repeat for opposite side.

Sashing Strip #6

Sashing Strip #5

Sashing Strip #4

Sashing Strip #3

Sashing Strip #2

Sashing Strip #1

Quilt Top Assembly Diagram

3. Join 1 Star block, 2 tan floral print M triangles, and 1 tan floral print N triangle to make border corner. Add to quilt. Repeat for remaining 3 corners.

4. Join 1 blue stripe sashing strip #6 to left side of quilt center. Repeat for opposite side. Join 1 red floral print O square to each end of 2 remaining sashing strip #6. Add strips to top and bottom of quilt.

Finishing

1. Divide backing fabric into 3 (3¼-yard) pieces. Join panels lengthwise.

2. Layer backing, batting, and quilt top; baste. Quilt as desired.

3. Join 2¼"-wide red dot strips into 1 continuous piece for straight-grain French-fold binding. Add binding to quilt.

TRIED & TRUE

Using bright geometric prints from Fabri-Quilt, Inc., we recreated the center of Marianne's quilt as a contemporary wallhanging.

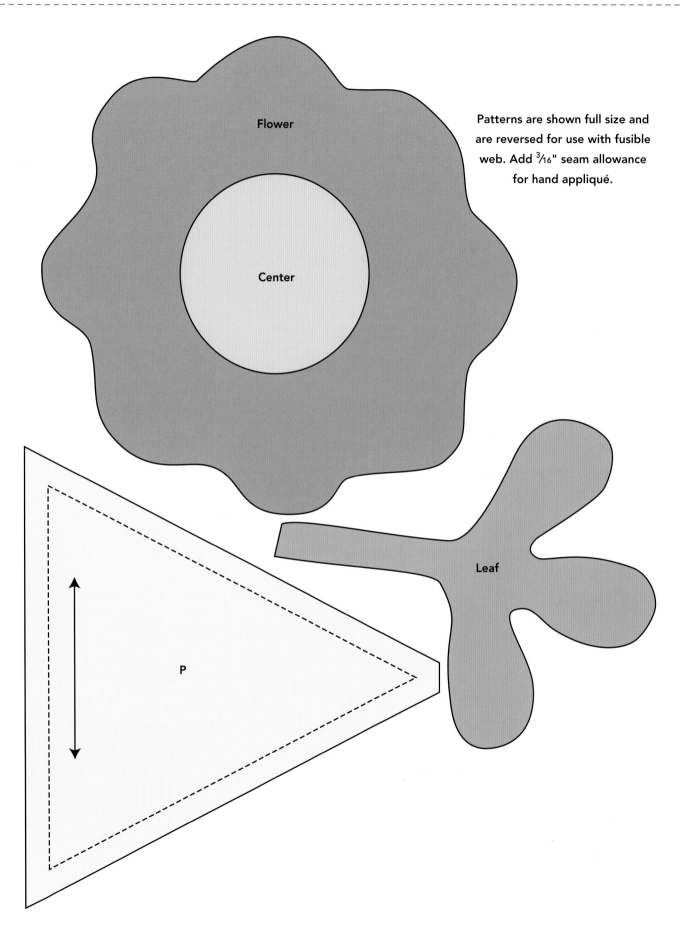

Patterns are shown full size and are reversed for use with fusible web. Add $\frac{3}{16}$" seam allowance for hand appliqué.

Making Flying Geese Units

The Fons & Porter Flying Geese Ruler takes the guesswork out of cutting the triangles for Flying Geese Units in finished sizes from 1" × 2" to 4" × 8". Both the large quarter-square triangle and the smaller half-square triangles are cut from the same width strips.

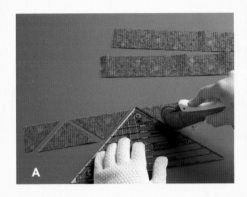

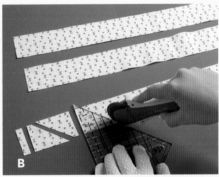

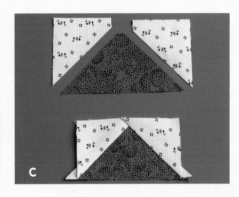

1. To cut the large quarter-square triangle, select black line on ruler that corresponds to the desired finished size Flying Geese Unit. (For the star points in *Our Home Sweet Home* on page 86, the finished size is 1½" × 3".)

2. Follow across black line to right edge of ruler and cut a fabric strip the width indicated. For example, to cut the large triangle for the 1½" × 3" finished-size Flying Geese Unit, cut a 2"-wide fabric strip.

3. Cut quarter-square triangles as shown in *Photo A*, first placing the black cutting guideline along bottom cut edge of strip and then along top edge of strip.

4. To cut the corresponding smaller half-square triangles, select the yellow line that corresponds to the desired finished size Flying Geese Unit.

5. Follow across yellow line to left edge of ruler and cut a fabric strip the width indicated. For example, to cut the small triangles for a 1½" × 3" finished-size Flying Geese Unit, cut a 4"-wide fabric strip.

6. Cut triangles as shown, first placing the yellow cutting guideline along bottom edge of strip and then along top edge (*Photo B*). The yellow shaded area of the ruler will extend beyond the edge of the strip.

Sew **Smart**™

Your triangles will be pre-trimmed with the tiny fabric tips that you usually cut off after sewing already eliminated. We cut these triangles with our strip folded in half so that half of our triangles are trimmed on the right end and the other half of them on the left end (*Photo C*). —Marianne

7. Join half-square triangles to center quarter-square triangle to complete 1 Flying Geese Unit.

Quick Triangle-Squares and Hourglass Units

Try our quick and easy method to make Triangle-Squares and Hourglass Units from squares. Use the Fons & Porter Quarter Inch Seam Markers to draw your stitching lines.

A

Triangle-Squares

1. From each of 1 light and 1 dark fabric, cut a square ⅞" larger than the desired finished size of the Triangle-Square. For example, to make a Triangle-Square that will finish 3", cut 3⅞" squares.

2. On the wrong side of light square, place the Quarter Inch Seam Marker diagonally across the square, with the yellow center line positioned exactly at corners. Mark stitching guidelines along both sides of the Quarter Inch Seam Marker (Photo A).

   NOTE: If you are not using the Fons & Porter Quarter Inch Seam Marker, draw a diagonal line from corner to corner across square. Then draw sewing lines on each side of the first line, ¼" away.

3. Place light square atop dark square, right sides facing; stitch along marked sewing lines.

4. Cut between rows of stitching to make two triangle-squares (Photo B). Press seams toward darker fabric.

Hourglass Units

1. From 1 light and 1 dark fabric, cut 1 square 1¼" larger than the desired finished size of the Hourglass Unit. For example, to make an Hourglass Unit that will finish 3", cut 4¼" squares.

2. Follow Steps #2–#4 to make 2 triangle-squares.

3. On the wrong side of one triangle-square, place Quarter Inch Seam Marker diagonally across square, perpendicular to seam, aligning yellow center line with corners of square. Mark stitching guidelines along both sides of Quarter Inch Seam Marker (Photo C). See **NOTE** in Step #2 if you are not using the Quarter Inch Seam Marker.

4. Place triangle square with drawn line atop matching triangle-square, right sides facing and opposite sides facing. Stitch along both drawn lines. Cut between stitching lines to create 2 Hourglass Units (Photo D). Press seam allowances to 1 side.

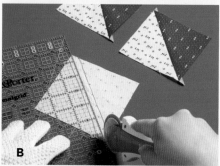

B

C

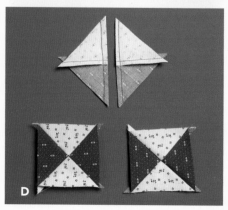

D

Cutting Setting Triangles

With the Fons & Porter Easy Diagonal Sets Ruler, cutting the side and corner setting triangles for diagonally set quilts is a snap—all the math is done for you! Cut side and corner setting triangles from the same size strip.

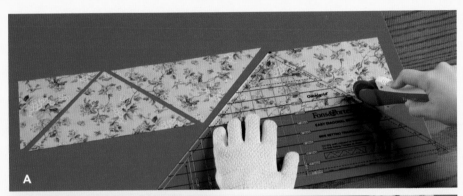

A

B

Cutting Corner Setting Triangles

1. On the Diagonal Sets Ruler, find the yellow line that corresponds to your finished block size.
2. Cut a strip that width.
3. Cut corner setting triangles from strip by first aligning the yellow cutting guideline along bottom edge of cut strip and then along top edge (Photo B).

Sew Smart™

Use the same width strip to cut both the side and corner setting triangles. If you are short on fabric, first cut a corner setting triangle (yellow lines) from the strip; then, cut the remainder of the strip into side setting triangles and finish by cutting a corner setting triangle.
—Liz

Cutting Side Setting Triangles

1. On the Diagonal Sets Ruler, find the black line that corresponds to your finished block size. The Star blocks in *Our Home Sweet Home* are 6" finished.
2. Cut a fabric strip the width indicated along the edge of the ruler. For the Star blocks in *Our Home Sweet Home*, cut strips 4¾" wide.

Sew Smart™

If your blocks finish in a fraction of an inch or you want to "float" your blocks in a diagonal set, use the next largest block size.
—Marianne

3. Open out strip so you will cut through a single layer. From strip, cut side setting triangles by first placing the black cutting guideline along bottom edge of strip, then top edge (Photo A).

Sew Easy™

Using Tri-Recs™ Tool

Follow our instructions for using a Tri-Recs™ tool to cut P triangles for the triangle border in *Our Home Sweet Home* on page 86.

Cutting Triangles

1. Cut 1 fabric strip the width needed for triangles. To determine strip size, add ½" to the desired finished height of the triangle. For example, for a 4" finished size triangle for the triangle border in *Our Home Sweet Home* on page 86, cut strips 4½" wide.

2. Position the Tri tool atop 1 strip, aligning the mark corresponding to your strip width along bottom edge of strip. Cut along both angled sides of Tri tool *(Photo A)*.

3. Reposition Tri tool with strip width line along top edge of strip and side of tool along previously cut edge. Cut another triangle *(Photo B)*. Continue in this manner to cut desired number of triangles.

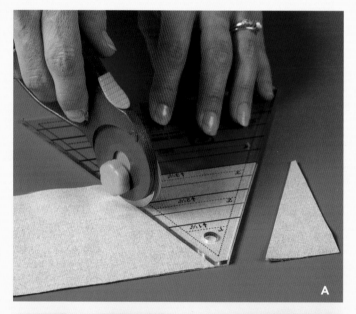

A

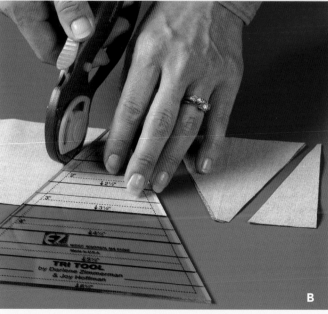

B

QUILT BY **Marianne Fons.**

Marianne's Flying Geese

A blue-and-white toile print from Marianne's stash was the inspiration for this quilt. The appliqué border is machine stitched.

PROJECT RATING: INTERMEDIATE

Size: 77" × 80½"

Blocks:

105 (3½" × 7") Flying Geese Units

MATERIALS

5 yards blue-and-white toile for setting strips and border

1⅞ yards cream print for Flying Geese Units

9 fat quarters★ assorted prints in tan, blue, gold, red, pink, and green for Flying Geese Units

1½ yards dark green print for vines, stems, and leaves

1 fat quarter★ each of gold, red, and blue prints for flowers

⅝ yard blue print for binding

5 yards backing fabric

Paper-backed fusible web

Fons & Porter Flying Geese Ruler (optional)

Full-size quilt batting

★fat quarter = 18" × 20"

Cutting

Measurements include ¼" seam allowances. Border strip is exact length needed. You may want to make it longer to allow for piecing variations. Patterns for appliqué are on page 103. Follow manufacturer's instructions for using fusible web. Refer to page 104 for instructions on using the Fons & Porter Flying Geese Ruler.

NOTE: Cutting Instructions are for use with the Fons & Porter Flying Geese Ruler. If you are NOT using this Ruler, read through all instructions carefully before beginning to cut.

From blue toile, cut:

• 2 (7½"-wide) strips. Piece strips to make 1 (7½" × 77½") bottom border.

• 3 (7½"-wide) **lengthwise** strips. From strips, cut 6 (7½" × 74") strips.

From cream print, cut:

• 14 (4"-wide) strips. From strips, cut 210 half-square B triangles using the Flying Geese Ruler.

NOTE: If **not** using the Fons & Porter Flying Geese Ruler, cut:

• 14 (4⅜"-wide) strips. From strips, cut 105 (4⅜") squares. Cut squares in half diagonally to make 210 half-square B triangles.

From each fat quarter, cut:

• 4 (4"-wide) strips. From strips, cut 12 quarter-square A triangles using the Flying Geese Ruler.

NOTE: If **not** using the Fons & Porter Flying Geese Ruler, cut:

• 2 (8¼"-wide) strips. From strips, cut 3 (8¼") squares. Cut squares in half diagonally in both directions to make 12 quarter-square A triangles.

From green print , cut:

• 500" of (1⅜"-wide) bias strips for vine and stems. Fold bias strips in thirds, press, and hand baste fold in place to prepare stems for appliqué.

• 80 Leaves.

From red print fat quarter, cut:

• 17 Flowers.

From blue print fat quarter, cut:

• 16 Flowers.

From gold print fat quarter, cut:

• 33 Centers.

From blue print, cut:

• 9 (2¼"-wide) strips for binding.

Flying Geese Assembly

1. Lay out 1 print A triangle and 2 cream print B triangles as shown in *Flying Geese Diagrams.*

Flying Geese Diagrams

2. Join triangles to complete 1 Flying Geese Unit. Make 105 Flying Geese Units.

Quilt Assembly

1. Lay out 21 Flying Geese Units as shown in *Quilt Top Assembly Diagram.*

Join to make 1 Flying Geese row. Make 5 Flying Geese rows.

2. Lay out Flying Geese rows and toile strips as shown in *Quilt Top Assembly Diagram.* Join rows to complete quilt center.

3. Add bottom border to quilt.

4. Arrange vine, stems, leaves, flowers and flower centers on bottom border and outermost toile rows. Machine appliqué pieces using matching thread.

Finishing

1. Divide backing fabric into 2 (2½-yard) lengths. Cut 1 piece in half lengthwise to make 2 narrow panels. Join 1 narrow panel to each side of wider panel; press seam allowances toward narrow panels.

2. Layer backing, batting, and quilt top; baste. Quilt as desired. Quilt shown was outline quilted around the appliqué, with the appliqué design in the toile strips, and in the ditch in the Flying Geese rows *(Quilting Diagram).*

3. Join 2¼"-wide blue print strips into 1 continuous piece for straight-grain French-fold binding. Add binding to quilt.

Quilting Diagram

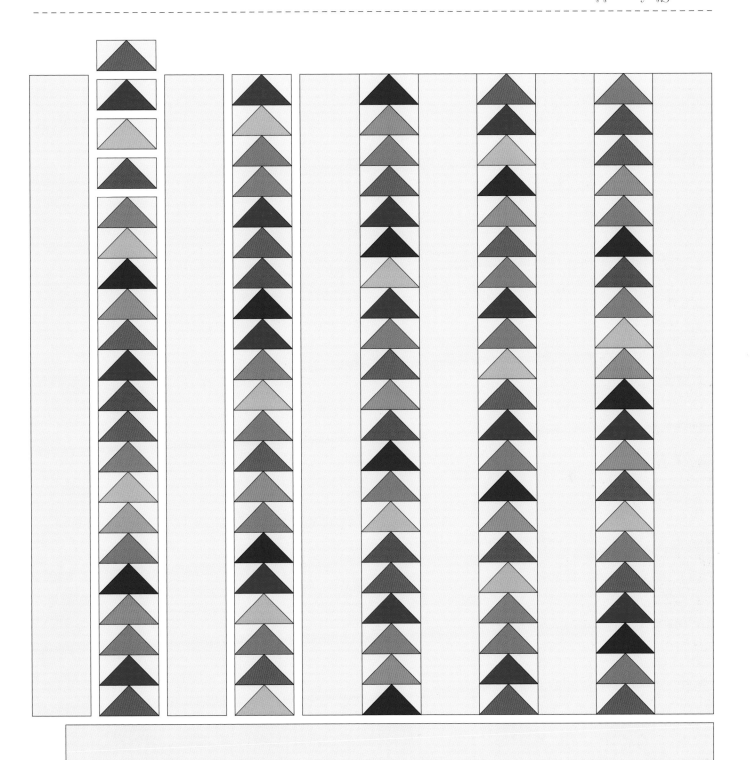

Quilt Top Assembly Diagram

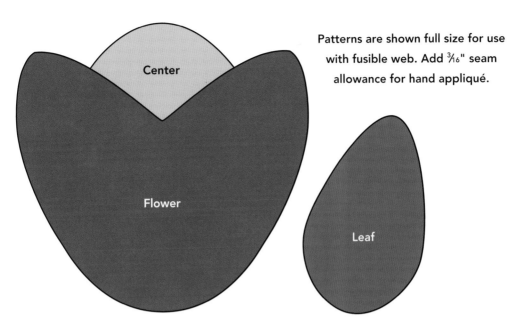

Center

Flower

Leaf

Patterns are shown full size for use with fusible web. Add ¾₆" seam allowance for hand appliqué.

TRIED & TRUE

Marianne's daughter Mary used contemporary fabrics to make a simplified version of this quilt. Instead of an appliqué vine, Mary used a large scale print to frame the Flying Geese.

Making Flying Geese Units

The Fons & Porter Flying Geese Ruler takes the guesswork out of cutting the triangles for Flying Geese Units in finished sizes from 1" × 2" to 4" × 8". Both the large quarter-square triangle and the smaller half-square triangles are cut from the same width strips.

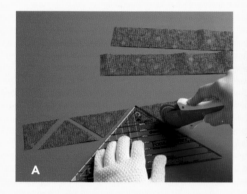

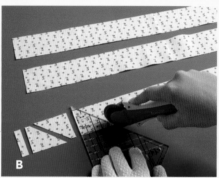

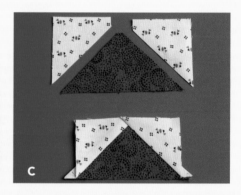

1. To cut the large quarter-square triangle, select black line on ruler that corresponds to the desired finished size Flying Geese Unit. (For *Marianne's Flying Geese* on page 98, the finished size is 3½" × 7".)

2. Follow across black line to right edge of ruler and cut a fabric strip the width indicated. For example, to cut the large triangle for the 3½" × 7" finished-size Flying Geese Unit, cut a 4"-wide fabric strip.

3. Cut quarter-square triangles as shown in *Photo A*, first placing the black cutting guideline along bottom cut edge of strip and then along top edge of strip.

4. To cut the corresponding smaller half-square triangles, select the yellow line that corresponds to the desired finished size Flying Geese Unit.

5. Follow across yellow line to left edge of ruler and cut a fabric strip the width indicated. For example, to cut the small triangles for a 3½" × 7" finished size Flying Geese Unit, cut a 4"-wide fabric strip.

6. Cut triangles as shown, first placing the yellow cutting guideline along bottom edge of strip and then along top edge (*Photo B*). The yellow shaded area of the ruler will extend beyond the edge of the strip.

Sew **Smart**™

Your triangles will be pre-trimmed with the tiny fabric tips that you usually cut off after sewing already eliminated. We cut these triangles with our strip folded in half so that half of our triangles are trimmed on the right end and the other half of them on the left end (*Photo C*).
—Marianne

7. Join half-square triangles to quarter-square triangle to complete 1 Flying Geese Unit.

Flying Geese Mini

Size: 15" × 19½"

Blocks: 39 (1½" × 3") Flying Geese
units

MATERIALS

¼ yard tan print

1 fat quarter★★ cream print

5 fat eighths★ assorted prints in
gold, red, blue, pink, and green
for Flying Geese

¼ yard blue print for binding

½ yard backing fabric

Fons & Porter Flying Geese ruler
(optional)

18" × 24" piece quilt batting

★fat eighth = 9" × 20"

★★fat quarter = 18" × 20"

Cutting

Measurements include ¼" seam allowances.

**NOTE: Cutting Instructions are for use
with the Fons & Porter Flying Geese
Ruler. If you are NOT using the Fons
& Porter Flying Geese Ruler, read
through all instructions carefully before
beginning to cut.**

From tan print, cut:

• 1 (3½"-wide) strip. From strip, cut 2
(3½" × 20") strips.

From cream print, cut:

• 7 (2"-wide) strips. From strips, cut 78
half-square B triangles using the Flying
Geese Ruler.

NOTE: If **not** using the Fons &
Porter Flying Geese Ruler, cut:

• 6 (2⅜"-wide) strips. From strips,
cut 39 (2⅜") squares. Cut squares
in half diagonally to make 78
half-square B triangles.

From each fat eighth, cut:

• 2 (2"-wide) strips. From strips,
cut 8 quarter-square A triangles
using the Flying Geese Ruler.

NOTE: If **not** using the Fons &
Porter Flying Geese Ruler,
cut:

• 1 (4¼"-wide) strip. From
strip, cut 2 (4¼") squares.
Cut squares in half diagonally in both directions to
make 8 quarter-square
A triangles.

From blue print, cut:

• 2 (2¼"-wide) strips for
binding.

Flying Geese Assembly

1. Lay out 1 A triangle and 2 cream
print B triangles as shown in *Flying
Geese Diagrams* on page 100.

2. Join triangles to complete 1 Flying
Geese Unit. Make 39 Flying Geese
Units.

Quilt Assembly

1. Lay out 13 Flying Geese Units as
shown in photo. Join to make 1 Flying
Geese row. Make 3 Flying Geese rows.

2. Lay out Flying Geese rows and tan
print strips as shown. Join rows to
complete quilt top.

Finishing

1. Layer backing, batting, and quilt top;
baste. Quilt as desired. Quilt shown
was quilted in the ditch in the Flying
Geese rows and with a gentle curve in
the tan strips.

2. Join 2¼"-wide blue print strips into
1 continuous piece for straight-grain
French-fold binding. Add binding to
quilt.

QUILT BY **Marianne Fons.**
MACHINE QUILTED BY **Dawn Cavanaugh**.

Blue Streak

Marianne loves traditional quilts that look great but are easy to make. Because the Split Nine Patch blocks have a light and a dark half, you can set them in any Log Cabin arrangement. Marianne chose Streak o' Lightning.

PROJECT RATING: EASY
Size: 68" × 80"
Blocks: 120 (6") Split Nine Patch blocks

MATERIALS

13 fat quarters★ blue prints
13 fat quarters★ shirting prints
¾ yard red print for center squares
1¾ yards blue print for border and binding
Fons & Porter Quarter Inch Seam Marker (optional)
5 yards backing fabric
Twin-size quilt batting
★fat quarter = 18" × 20"

NOTE: Fabrics in the quilt shown are from the Farmhouse Blues collection by L.B. Krueger for Windham Fabrics.

Cutting

Measurements include ¼" seam allowances. Border strips are exact length needed. You may want to make them longer to allow for piecing variations.

From each blue and shirting print fat quarter, cut:
• 2 (2⅞"-wide) strips. From strips, cut 10 (2⅞") A squares.
• 4 (2½"-wide) strips. From strips, cut 28 (2½") B squares.

From red print, cut:
• 8 (2½"-wide) strips. From strips, cut 120 (2½") B squares.

From blue print, cut:
• 8 (4½"-wide) strips. Piece strips to make 2 (4½" × 72½") side borders and 2 (4½" × 68½") top and bottom borders.
• 8 (2¼"-wide) strips for binding.

Block Assembly

> ### Sew Smart™
>
> To make triangle-squares using the Fons & Porter Quarter Inch Seam Markers, see *Sew Easy: Quick Triangle-Squares* on page 139.
> —Marianne

1. Referring to *Triangle-Square Diagrams*, draw a diagonal line on wrong side of 1 shirting print A square. Place marked square atop 1 blue print A square, right sides facing. Stitch ¼" on each side of drawn line as shown. Cut on drawn line to make 2 triangle-squares. Press seam allowances toward blue fabric. Make 240 triangle-squares.

Triangle-Square Diagrams

2. Referring to *Block Assembly Diagram*, lay out 1 red print B square, 3 shirting print B squares, 3 blue print B squares, and 2 triangle-squares. Join into rows; join rows to complete 1 Split Nine Patch block (*Block Diagram*). Make 120 blocks.

Block Assembly Diagram

Block Diagram

Quilt Assembly

1. Lay out blocks as shown in *Quilt Top Assembly Diagram*. Join into rows; join rows to complete quilt center.
2. Add side borders to quilt center. Add top and bottom borders to quilt.

Finishing

1. Divide backing fabric into 2 (2½-yard) pieces. Divide 1 piece in half lengthwise to make 2 narrow panels.

Join 1 narrow panel to each side of wider panel; press seam allowances toward narrow panels.

2. Layer backing, batting, and quilt top; baste. Quilt as desired. Quilt shown has feathers in light areas and zigzag lines in dark areas (*Quilting Diagram*).
3. Join 2¼"-wide blue print strips into 1 continuous piece for straight-grain French-fold binding. Add binding to quilt.

Quilt Top Assembly Diagram

SIZE OPTIONS

	Crib (44" × 56")	Full (80" × 98")	Queen (92" × 104")
Blocks	48	180	224
Setting	6 × 8 blocks	12 × 15 blocks	14 × 16 blocks

MATERIALS

	Crib (44" × 56")	Full (80" × 98")	Queen (92" × 104")
Blue Prints	6 fat quarters	20 fat quarters	24 fat quarters
Shirting Prints	6 fat quarters	20 fat quarters	24 fat quarters
Red Print	½ yard	1 yard	1¼ yards
Blue Border and Binding Print	1⅛ yards	1⅞ yards	2⅛ yards
Backing Fabric	2¾ yards	7½ yards	8½ yards
Batting	Twin-size	Queen-size	King-size

CUTTING

	Crib (44" × 56")	Full (80" × 98")	Queen (92" × 104")
Each Light and Dark Fat Quarter	2 ($2\frac{7}{8}$" × 20") strips. From strips, cut 8 ($2\frac{7}{8}$") A squares.	2 ($2\frac{7}{8}$" × 20") strips. From strips, cut 9 ($2\frac{7}{8}$") A squares.	2 ($2\frac{7}{8}$" × 20") strips. From strips, cut 10 ($2\frac{7}{8}$") A squares.
	3 (2½"-wide) strips. From strips, cut 24 (2½") B squares.	4 (2½"-wide) strips. From strips, cut 27 (2½") B squares.	4 (2½"-wide) strips. From strips, cut 28 (2½") B squares.
Red Print	3 (2½"-wide) strips. From strips, cut 48 (2½") B squares.	12 (2½"-wide) strips. From strips, cut 180 (2½") B squares.	12 (2½"-wide) strips. From strips, cut 224 (2½") B squares.
Blue Border	5 (4½"-wide) strips.	9 (4½"-wide) strips.	10 (4½"-wide) strips.
Binding	6 (2¼"-wide) strips.	10 (2¼"-wide) strips.	11 (2¼"-wide) strips.

Quilting Diagram

TRIED & TRUE

Tonal prints in green with a splash of purple give this version a watercolor look. Fabrics shown are from the Four Seasons collection by Jinny Beyer for RJR Fabrics. ✳

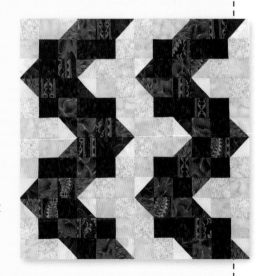

Sunset Sail

Marianne used beautiful Indonesian batiks in ocean blues and greens to make this Split Nine Patch quilt variation with a Barn Raising setting for her daughter Rebecca who loves sailing.

PROJECT RATING: EASY
Size: 83" × 107"
Blocks: 192 (6") Split Nine
Patch blocks

MATERIALS

22 fat quarters★ blue batiks
22 fat quarters★ green batiks
1 yard dark pink batik
2½ yards dark blue batik for border
  and binding
7½ yards backing fabric
Fons & Porter Quarter Inch Seam
  Marker (optional)
Queen-size quilt batting
★fat quarter = 18" × 20"

NOTE: Fabrics in the quilt shown are from the Tonga Batiks collection by Timeless Treasures.

Cutting

Measurements include ¼" seam allowances. Border strips are exact length needed. You may want to make them longer to allow for piecing variations.
From each fat quarter, cut:
• 2 (2⅞"-wide) strips. From strips, cut 9 (2⅞") A squares.
• 4 (2½"-wide) strips. From strips, cut 27 (2½") B squares.

From dark pink batik, cut:
• 12 (2½"-wide) strips. From strips, cut 192 (2½") B squares.

From dark blue batik, cut:
• 10 (6"-wide) strips. Piece strips to make 2 (6" × 96½") side borders and 2 (6" × 83½") top and bottom borders.

• 11 (2¼"-wide) strips for binding

Quilt Assembly instructions are on page 108.

Quilt Top Assembly Diagram

QUILT BY **Marianne Fons.**
MACHINE QUILTED BY **Dawn Cavanaugh.**

Grandmother's Flowerpots

An anonymous quilter from the 1930s or '40s
started this quilt by making a set of pretty flower blocks.
When Marianne discovered them at a quilt show booth,
she instantly knew exactly how she wanted to set them together.
"I only wish I could thank the woman who 'pre-started'
this project for me!" says Marianne.

PROJECT RATING: INTERMEDIATE
Size: 81" × 104"
Blocks: 18 (14") Flowerpot blocks

MATERIALS

27 fat quarters★ assorted 1930s
   reproduction prints in red, yellow,
   green, blue, pink, and lavender
   for flowers, sashing, and outer
   borders
5 yards white solid for block
   background, sashing, and setting
   triangles
2 yards yellow solid for flower
   centers, sashing squares, inner
   border, and binding
¾ yard teal solid for flowerpots and
   flower stems
Card stock for English paper
   piecing
Lightweight fusible interfacing
   (optional)
Temporary spray adhesive (optional)
7½ yards backing fabric
Queen-size quilt batting
★fat quarter = 18" × 20"

Cutting

Measurements include ¼" seam allowances. Border strips are exact length needed. You may want to make them longer to allow for piecing variations. Patterns for hexagon and flowerpot are on page 119.

From each of 18 fat quarters, cut:

• 1 (7⅞"-wide) strip. From strip, cut 2 (7⅞") squares. Cut squares in half diagonally to make 4 half-square A triangles.

• 1 (2⅞"-wide) strip. From strip, cut 6 (2⅞") squares. Cut squares in half diagonally to make 12 half-square B triangles.

• 2 (1½"-wide) strips for strips sets.

• 12 Hexagons (See *Sew Easy: English Paper Piecing* on page 117 for cutting instructions.)

From each of remaining 9 fat quarters, cut:

• 2 (2⅞"-wide) strips. From strips, cut 7 (2⅞") squares. Cut squares in half diagonally to make 14 half-square B triangles.

• 6 (1½"-wide) strips for strip sets.

From white solid, cut:

• 3 (21"-wide) strips. From strips, cut 3 (21") squares and 2 (10¾") squares. Cut 21" squares in half diagonally in both directions to make 12 side setting triangles (2 are extra). Cut 10¾" squares in half diagonally to make 4 corner setting triangles.

• 6 (10⅜"-wide) strips. From strips, cut 18 (10⅜") squares for block backgrounds.

• 13 (2⅞"-wide) strips. From strips, cut 168 (2⅞") squares. Cut squares in half diagonally to make 336 half-square B triangles.

From yellow solid, cut:

• 1 (5"-wide) strip. From strip, cut 4 (5") border corner squares.

• 11 (2½"-wide) strips. Piece 9 strips to make 2 (2½" × 91½") side inner borders and 2 (2½" × 72½") top and bottom inner borders. From remaining strips, cut 31 (2½") sashing squares.

• 10 (2¼"-wide) strips for binding.

• 36 Hexagons (See *Sew Easy: English Paper Piecing* on page 117 for cutting instructions.).

From teal solid, cut:

• 1 (2½"-wide) strip. From strip cut 36 (¾"-wide) bias strips for stems.

• 18 Flowerpots.

Block Assembly

1. Referring to *Sew Easy: English Paper Piecing* on page 117, join 6 matching print hexagons and 1 yellow hexagon to complete 1 flower. Make 36 flowers.

2. Fold teal bias stem strips in thirds and press to make ¼"-wide stems. Loosely hand baste along center of each stem to hold edges in place.

3. Arrange 2 matching flowers, 2 stems, and 1 flowerpot on white background square as shown in *Block Diagram*. See *Sew Easy: Interfacing Appliqué* on page 118 for an easy way to prepare flowerpots for appliqué.
Appliqué stems, flowers, and flower-

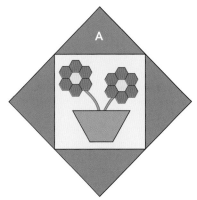

Block Diagram

pots to background.

4. Choose 4 matching A triangles; join 1 triangle to each side of background square to complete 1 Flowerpot block *(Block Diagram)*. Make 18 Flowerpot blocks.

Sashing Assembly

1. Join 1 print B triangle and 1 white B triangle as shown in *Triangle-Square*

Triangle-Square Diagrams

Diagrams. Make 336 triangle-squares.

2. Join 7 triangle-squares as shown to make 1 Unit A *(Unit A Diagram)*.

Unit A Diagram

Make 24 Unit A.

3. In the same manner, make 24 Unit B *(Unit B Diagram)*.

Unit B Diagram

Quilt Assembly

1. Lay out blocks, sashing units, sashing squares, side setting triangles, and corner setting triangles as shown in *Quilt Top Assembly Diagram*.

2. Join into diagonal rows; join rows to complete quilt center. Trim corners of sashing squares even with edges of quilt center.

3. Add yellow side inner borders to quilt center. Add yellow top and bottom inner borders to quilt.

4. Join 5 (1½"-wide) print strips as shown in *Strip Set Diagram*. Make 18 strip sets. From strip sets, cut 68 (5"-wide) segments.

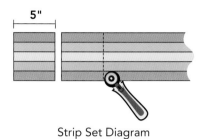

Strip Set Diagram

5. Join 19 strip set segments as shown in *Quilt Top Assembly Diagram* to make 1 side outer border. Make 2 side borders; add borders to sides of quilt center.

6. Join 15 strip set segments to make top outer border. Remove 3 strips from border to adjust to correct length. Repeat for bottom border.

7. Add 1 (5") yellow corner square to each end of top and bottom outer borders. Add borders to quilt.

Finishing

1. Divide backing fabric into 3 (2½-yard) pieces. Join pieces lengthwise. Seams will run horizontally.

2. Layer backing, batting, and quilt top; baste. Quilt as desired. Quilt shown was quilted with a diagonal grid in block background, flower and leaf designs in block triangles, feathers in setting triangles, leaves in yellow borders, and in the ditch in outer borders.

3. Join 2¼"-wide yellow strips into 1 continuous piece for straight-grain French-fold binding. Add binding to quilt.

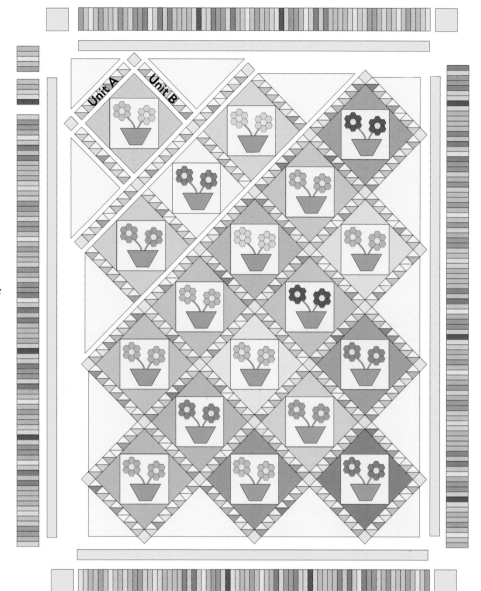

Quilt Top Assembly Diagram

TRIED & TRUE

We made a country version from the Vintage Stitches line by Thimbleberries® for RJR Fabrics✳

English Paper Piecing

This easy method for English paper piecing uses card stock and spray temporary adhesive, eliminating the need for hand basting.

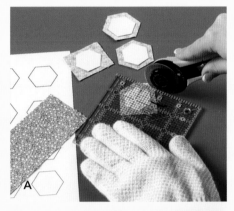

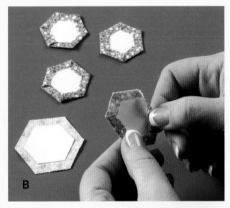

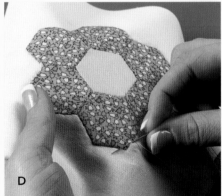

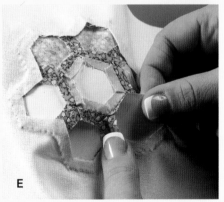

Sew **Smart**™

When using spray adhesive, place fabric pieces inside a cardboard box to keep the spray adhesive from accumulating on work surfaces.
—Marianne

1. Cut hexagons from card stock, using pattern on page 119. You will need 7 for each flower.
2. Lightly spray card stock hexagons with temporary adhesive and place atop wrong side of fabric. Cut around hexagons, adding ¼" seam allowance as you cut (Photo A). Cut 6 matching print hexagons and 1 yellow solid hexagon for each flower.

3. Lightly spray wrong side of fabric and card stock hexagons with spray temporary fabric adhesive. Turn seam allowance over card stock around each piece (Photo B).
4. Whipstitch hexagons together, catching fabric edges but not card stock (Photo C). Make tiny stitches, approximately ¹⁄₁₆" to ⅛" apart, and sew from corner to corner. Knot thread or make

backstitches to secure whipstitched seam at beginning and end. Join 1 print hexagon to each side of yellow hexagon to complete 1 flower.
5. Appliqué flower to background (Photo D).
6. Cut background fabric from behind flower. Remove card stock hexagons (Photo E).

Sew Easy™

Interfacing Appliqué

For large shapes with fairly smooth edges, this appliqué technique works well. Fusing pieces to the background eliminates the need for basting.

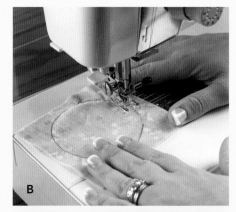

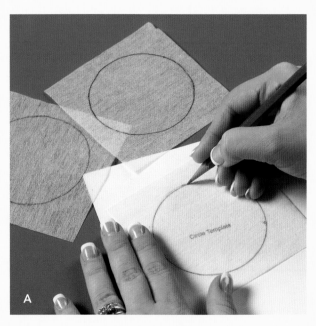

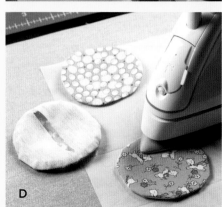

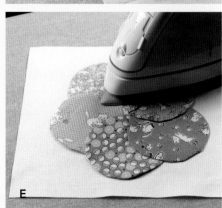

1. Trace appliqué shape onto fusible interfacing; cut out about ½" outside of drawn line (Photo A).
2. Position interfacing atop appliqué with fusible side of interfacing against right side of fabric. Stitch on drawn line through both layers (Photo B).
3. Trim away excess fabric, leaving a ¼" seam allowance. Cut a slit in interfacing to turn appliqué piece (Photo C).

4. Turn piece right side out, place on non-stick appliqué pressing sheet, and press shape flat (Photo D).
5. Lay out pieces on background fabric and fuse in place (Photo E).
6. Appliqué pieces to background using either a hand or machine stitch.

Sew Smart™

For curved pieces, clip curves OR trim seam allowance with pinking shears to make the piece lie flat when it is turned right side out. —Marianne

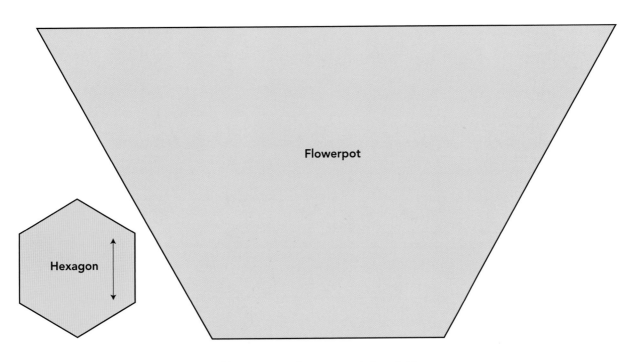

Patterns are shown actual size. Add
³⁄₁₆" seam allowance for hand appliqué.

QUILT BY **Liz Porter.**
MACHINE QUILTED BY **Kelly Ashton**.

Batik Fans

Liz adopted some orphan blocks left over from a TV episode and added to them to complete a terrific quilt in no time at all. Strip sets make the border go together quickly as well.
See *Sew Easy: Making Nine-Blade Fan Blocks* on page 125 for instructions on cutting patchwork pieces using our special template set.

PROJECT RATING: INTERMEDIATE
Size: 58½" × 84"
Blocks: 40 (8½") Fan blocks

MATERIALS

35 fat quarters★ assorted bright batiks for blocks and border
2½ yards lavender print for block backgrounds
⅝ yard purple batik for binding
Nine-Blade Fan Template Set or template material
5 yards backing fabric
Twin-size quilt batting
Tailor's chalk
★fat quarter = 18" × 20"

Cutting

Note: Cutting for this quilt is tricky. Be sure to read *Sew Easy: Making Nine-Blade Fan Blocks* on page 125 before beginning.

If you do not have the Nine Blade Fan Template Set, make templates from patterns on page 124. Measurements include ¼" seam allowances.

From each fat quarter, cut:

• 12 Fan Blades. (You will have a few extra.)

• 4 (1½"-wide) strips for strip sets.

From remainder of each of 4 fat quarters, cut:

• 1 Center.

From lavender print, cut:

• 40 Backgrounds.

• 40 Centers.

From purple batik, cut:

• 8 (2¼"-wide) strips for binding.

Fan Block Assembly

1. Refer to *Sew Easy: Making Nine-Blade Fan Blocks* on page 125 to complete 1 Fan block *(Fan Block*

Fan Block Diagram

Diagram). Make 40 Fan blocks.

2. In a similar manner, make 4 Corner blocks with bright centers and without background piece *(Corner Block Diagram)*.

Corner Block Diagram

Quilt Assembly

1. Referring to photo on page 123, lay out Fan blocks as shown. Join into horizontal rows; join rows to complete quilt center.

2. Join 8 (1½"-wide) bright strips as shown in *Strip Set Diagram*. Make 15 strip sets. From strip sets, cut 28 (8½"-wide) segments.

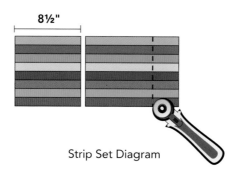

8½"

Strip Set Diagram

3. Join 9 segments to make 1 side border. Trim as needed to adjust border length to fit quilt center. Repeat for other side border. Add side borders to quilt center.

4. Join 5 segments to make top border. Trim as needed to adjust border length to fit quilt center. Add 1 corner block to each end of border. Repeat for bottom border. Add borders to quilt.

Finishing

1. Divide backing into 2 (2½-yard) lengths. Cut 1 piece in half lengthwise to make 2 narrow panels. Join 1 narrow panel to each side of wider panel. Press seam allowances toward narrow panel.

2. Layer backing, batting, and quilt top; baste. Quilt as desired. Quilt shown was quilted with spirals in the fan centers, a petal design in the fan blades, and feathers in the block backgrounds and borders.

3. Join 2¼"-wide purple batik strips into 1 continuous piece for straight-grain French-fold binding.

4. Draw a gentle curved line along the raw edge of the pieced border. Stitch binding to quilt along chalk line. Trim border; turn binding to back, and whipstitch in place.

TRIED & TRUE

Arrange four fan blocks in a circle for a different look. Fabrics shown are from the Civil War III Circa 1860 collection by Windham Fabrics. ✳

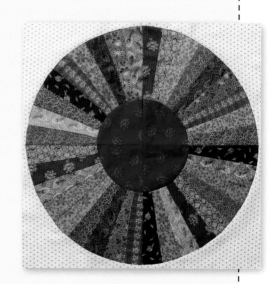

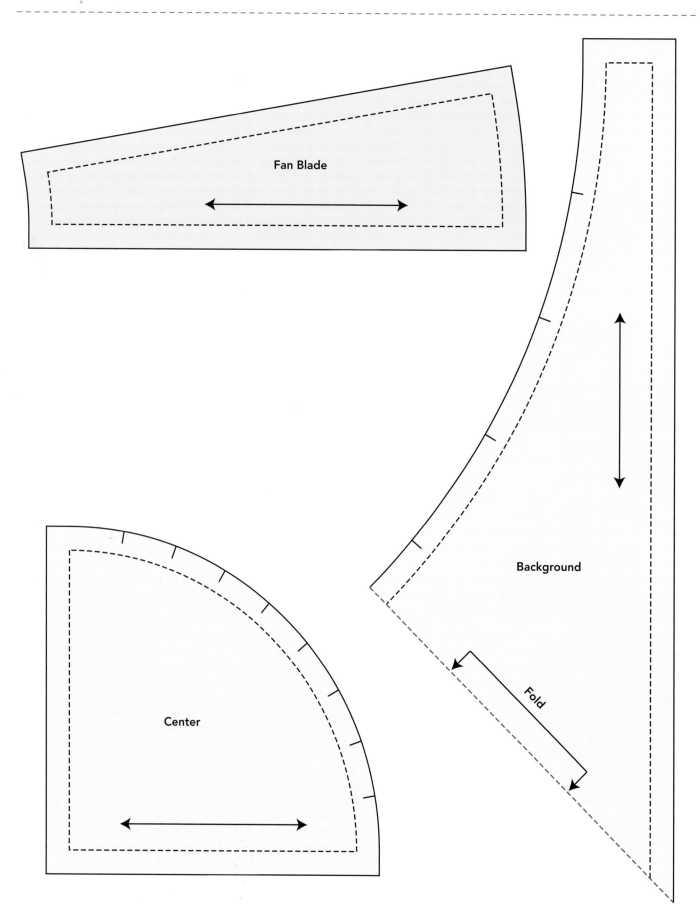

Fan Blade

Background

Fold

Center

Making Nine-Blade Fan Blocks

Our Nine-Blade Fan Template Set and a small rotary cutter make cutting the pieces for 8½" fan blocks fast and easy. Stitch fan blocks into the *Batik Fans* quilt on page 120, or create your own design.

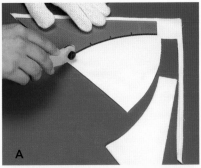
A

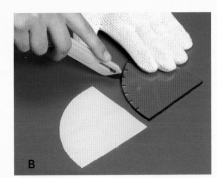
B

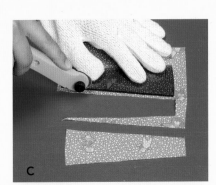
C

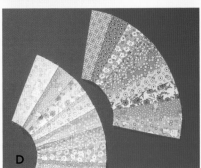
D

E

F

Cutting

1. From background fabric, cut 10½"-wide strips. From strips, cut 10½" squares. You can cut 2 background pieces from each square.
2. Fold background square in half diagonally. Align fold edge of template with fold of background square and cut 1 background piece. Flip template over and cut a second piece from background square (*Photo A*). Use a point cutting tool to make small notches in background pieces (*Photo B*). **NOTE:** If not using Template Set, make small notches in background pieces at marks indicated on patterns.

3. Using center template, cut 1 center piece for each fan unit. Use a point cutting tool to mark the notches.
4. Cut 5½"-wide strips from fabrics for blades. Cut 9 blades for each fan unit, using blade template and rotating it on strip after each cut (*Photo C*).

Assembly

1. Join 9 fan blades. Press all seam allowances in one direction (*Photo D*).
2. Place blade unit atop center piece, right sides together. Align seams in blade unit with notches in center piece. Place a pin at each end and at 1 or 2 of the notches in center of piece.

With blade unit on top, stitch ¼" seam (*Photo E*). Press seam allowance toward center piece.

3. Place background piece atop blade unit, right sides together. Align seams in blade unit with notches in background piece. Place a pin at each end and at 1 or 2 of the notches in center of piece. With background piece on top, stitch ¼" seam (*Photo F*). Press seam allowance toward background piece.

Petite Baskets

Marianne made this adorable miniature quilt using fabrics she has collected on trips to Provence, France, and at quilt shops around the US.

PROJECT RATING: INTERMEDIATE
Size: 24½" × 30"
Blocks: 12 (4") Basket blocks
6 (4") Flower blocks

MATERIALS

1 fat quarter★★ white print for block backgrounds
1 fat quarter★★ blue plaid for setting blocks
¼ yard blue stripe for inner border
⅝ yard red print for outer border and binding
1 fat quarter★★ yellow print for setting triangles
4 fat eighths★ in yellow, blue, red, and green prints for blocks
⅞ yard backing fabric
Paper-backed fusible web
6 (⅜"-diameter) yellow buttons
28" × 34" piece of quilt batting
★★fat quarter = 18" × 20"
★fat eighth = 9" × 20"

Cutting

Measurements include ¼" seam allowances. Border strips are exact length needed. You may want to make them longer to allow for piecing variations. Patterns for appliqué are on page 129.

Follow manufacturer's instructions for using fusible web.

From white print fat quarter, cut:
- 1 (2⅞"-wide) strip. From strip, cut 6 (2⅞") squares. Cut squares in half diagonally to make 12 half-square B triangles.
- 2 (2½"-wide) strips. From strips, cut 24 (2½" × 1½") C rectangles.
- 3 (1⅞"-wide) strips. From strips, cut 24 (1⅞") squares. Cut squares in half diagonally to make 48 half-square A triangles.
- 1 (1½"-wide) strip. From strip, cut 12 (1½") D squares.

From blue plaid fat quarter, cut:
- 2 (4½"-wide) strips. From strips, cut 6 (4½") E squares.

From blue stripe, cut:
- 3 (1¼"-wide) strips. From strips, cut 2 (1¼" × 23⅛") side inner borders and 2 (1¼" × 17½") top and bottom inner borders.

From red print, cut:
- 3 (3½"-wide) strips. From strips, cut 2 (3½" × 24⅝") side outer borders and 2 (3½" × 19") top and bottom outer borders.
- 4 (2¼"-wide) strips for binding.

From yellow print fat quarter, cut:
- 2 (7"-wide) strips. From strip, cut 3 (7") squares and 2 (3¾") squares. Cut 7" squares in half diagonally in both directions to make 12 side setting triangles (2 are extra). Cut 3¾" squares in half diagonally to make 4 corner setting triangles.

From yellow print fat eighth, cut:
- 1 (3½"-wide) strip. From strip, cut 4 (3½") F squares and 3 (2⅞") squares. Cut 2⅞" squares in half diagonally to make 6 half-square B triangles.
- 1 (1⅞"-wide) strip. From strip, cut 9 (1⅞") squares. Cut squares in half diagonally to make 18 half-square A triangles.

From each blue, red, and green print fat eighth, cut:
- 1 (2⅞"-wide) strip. From strip, cut 3 (2⅞") squares. Cut squares in half diagonally to make 6 half-square B triangles.
- 1 (1⅞"-wide) strip. From strip, cut 9 (1⅞") squares. Cut squares in half diagonally to make 18 half-square A triangles.

From remainder of red print fat eighth, cut:
- 6 Flowers.
- 4 (1¼") G squares.

From remainder of green print fat eighth, cut:
- 6 Leaves.

Block Assembly

1. Separate the red, yellow, green, and blue A triangles into 12 matching sets of 4 and 12 matching sets of 2.

2. Choose 1 matching set of 4 print A triangles. Join 1 print A triangle and 1 white print A triangle to make a small triangle-square *(Triangle-Square Diagrams)*. Make 4 triangle-squares.

Triangle-Square Diagrams

3. Join 2 print B triangles to make a large triangle-square.

4. Choose 1 matching set of 2 print A triangles. Join 1 print A triangle and 1 white print C rectangle to make 1 side unit *(Side Unit Diagrams)*. Make 1 side unit and 1 side unit reversed.

Side Unit Diagrams

5. Referring to *Basket Block Assembly Diagram*, lay out large triangle-square, 4 small triangle-squares, 1 white print D square, 1 white print B triangle, and 2 side units as shown. Join units to make 1 Basket block *(Basket Block Diagram)*. Make 12 Basket blocks.

Basket Block Assembly Diagram

Basket Block Diagram

6. Referring to *Flower Block Diagram*, fuse 1 Leaf and 1 Flower to 1 blue plaid E square. Machine appliqué using yellow thread. Sew a button to center of flower to complete 1 Flower block. Make 6 Flower blocks.

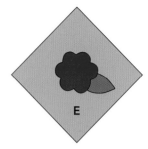

Flower Block Diagram

Quilt Assembly

1. Lay out Basket blocks, Flower blocks, and setting triangles as shown in *Quilt Top Assembly Diagram*. Join into diagonal rows; join rows to complete quilt center.

Quilt Top Assembly Diagram

2. Add blue stripe side inner borders to quilt center. Add 1 red print G square to each end of blue stripe top and bottom inner borders. Add borders to quilt.

3. Add red print side outer borders to quilt. Add 1 yellow print F square to each end of red floral top and bottom outer borders. Add borders to quilt.

Finishing

1. Layer backing, batting, and quilt top; baste. Quilt as desired. Quilt shown was quilted in the ditch around baskets, with echo quilting in Flower blocks and setting triangles, and with scalloped lines in outer border *(Quilting Diagram)*.

2. Join 2¼"-wide red print strips into 1 continuous piece for straight-grain French-fold binding. Add binding to quilt.

Quilting Diagram

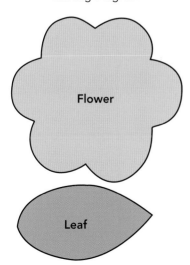

Flower

Leaf

TRIED & TRUE

A large floral print gives a more formal look to this wallhanging. We used The English Manor collection by RJR Fabrics. ✳

QUILT BY **Liz Porter.**
MACHINE QUILTED BY **Kelly Ashton**.

Blue Lagoon

Liz dug into her batik stash to create this big,
beautiful quilt. She says, "The batiks available today are so
gorgeous, picking up the strips to make the strip sets for the
pieced diamonds was like eating chocolates
from a candy box!"

PROJECT RATING: INTERMEDIATE
Size: 93⅜" × 90"

MATERIALS

3 yards light blue batik for pyramids
   and diamonds
3¾ yards dark blue batik for
   triangles, diamonds, and binding
¼ yard (9" × 40") each of 25
   assorted batiks for pieced
   diamonds
Fons & Porter 60° Pyramids Ruler
   or template material
Fons & Porter 60° Diamonds Ruler
Rotary cutting ruler with 60-degree
   angle lines
8¼ yards backing fabric
King-size quilt batting

Cutting

Measurements include ¼" seam allowances. Refer to *Sew Easy: Cutting 60° Diamonds and Pyramids* on page 135 for instructions on cutting diamonds and pyramids. If you are not using the Fons & Porter Pyramids Ruler, the pattern for pyramid is on page 134.

From light blue batik, cut:

• 17 (5½"-wide) strips. From strips, cut 16 Pyramids and 72 Diamonds.

Sew Smart™

If you are not using the Fons & Porter 60° Diamonds Ruler, use a regular ruler to trim end of strip at 60-degree angle. Position line on ruler that corresponds to the strip width on the angled edge. Cut along edge of ruler to make 1 diamond. Continue in this manner to cut desired number of diamonds.

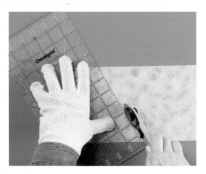

From dark blue batik, cut:

• 17 (5½"-wide) strips. From strips, cut 16 Pyramids and 72 Diamonds.

• 10 (2¼"-wide) strips for binding.

From each ¼-yard piece, cut:

• Crosswise strips ranging in width from 1¼"–2¼" for strip sets.

Strip Set Assembly and Cutting

1. Referring to *Strip Set Diagram*, join strips randomly by color and width into strip sets about 6" wide. Make 25 strip sets.

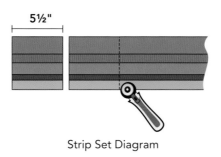

Strip Set Diagram

2. Referring to *Sew Easy: Cutting 60-Degree Diamonds and Pyramids* on page 135, cut 160 Pyramids from 15 of the strip sets.

3. Cut 7 (5½"-wide) segments from each of the remaining strip sets for pieced border.

Quilt Assembly

1. Referring to *Quilt Top Assembly Diagram*, join 2 dark blue Pyramids, 4 dark blue diamonds, 5 light blue diamonds, and 10 strip set Pyramids to complete Row 1. Make 8 Row 1.

2. Lay out 2 light blue Pyramids, 4 light blue Diamonds, 5 dark blue Diamonds, and 10 strip set Pyramids. Join pieces to complete Row 2. Make 8 Row 2.

3. Join rows, alternating Row 1 and Row 2, to complete quilt center. Straighten sides of quilt by trimming ¼" outside the pieced diamonds.

Row 1

Row 2

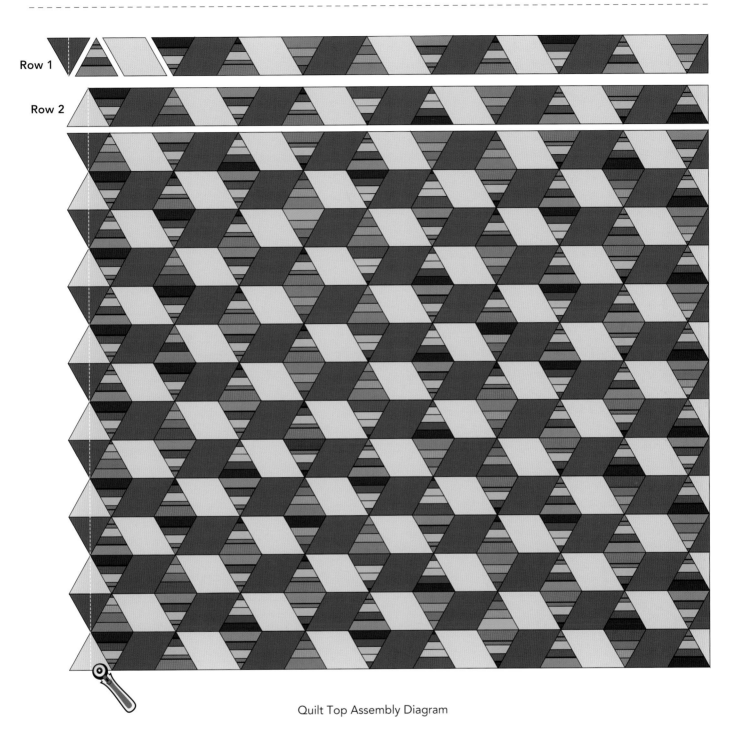

Quilt Top Assembly Diagram

4. Measure quilt length; join strip set segments to make 2 border strips this measurement. Add borders to quilt sides. Measure quilt width, including side borders; join strip set segments to make 2 border strips this measurement. Add borders to top and bottom of quilt top.

Quilting and Finishing

1. Divide backing fabric into 3 (2¾-yard) pieces. Join pieces lengthwise. Seams will run horizontally.

2. Layer backing, batting, and quilt top; baste. Quilt as desired. Quilt shown was quilted with flowers in the light

blue diamonds and border, and with a grid in the dark blue diamonds and pieced diamonds.

3. Join 2¼"-wide dark blue batik strips into 1 continuous piece for straight-grain French-fold binding. Add binding to quilt. ✳

Pyramid

Sew Easy™

Cutting 60° Diamonds and Pyramids

Use the Fons & Porter 60° Diamonds Ruler and 60° Pyramids Ruler to make easy work of cutting pieces for *Blue Lagoon* on page 130.

A

B

C

D

E

Diamonds

1. To cut diamonds, cut strip desired width (for *Blue Lagoon*, cut strips 5½" wide).

2. Referring to strip width numbers along lower section of Fons & Porter 60° Diamonds ruler, find the solid black line on the ruler that corresponds to the width of strip you cut.

3. Beginning at left end of fabric strip, place ruler so bottom solid line for desired size diamond is aligned with bottom edge of strip, and cut along left side of ruler (*Photo A*).

> ### Sew Smart™
> To cut the maximum number of pieces from a fabric strip, open out the strip so you will be cutting through a single layer. To cut many pieces, layer several strips and cut them at the same time. —Liz

4. Move ruler to the right; align desired line of ruler with slanted edge and bottom edge of strip. Cut along right slanted edge of ruler to cut diamond (*Photo B*).

5. Repeat Step #4 to cut required number of diamonds.

Pyramids

1. To cut pyramids, cut strip desired width (for *Blue Lagoon*, cut strips 5½" wide).

2. Referring to strip width numbers along lower section of Fons & Porter 60° Pyramids ruler, find the solid black line on the ruler that corresponds to the width of strip you cut.

3. Beginning at left end of fabric strip, place ruler atop strip so solid line on ruler is along bottom edge of fabric strip. Trim along left slanted edge of ruler.

> ### Sew Smart™
> If you cut left handed, work from the right end of the fabric strip and begin by cutting along the right edge of the ruler. —Marianne

4. Cut along right slanted edge of ruler to cut one pyramid triangle (*Photo C*).

5. To cut second pyramid triangle, rotate ruler so solid line is on top edge of strip and angled side of ruler is aligned with slanted edge of strip. Cut along slanted edge of ruler (*Photo D*).

4. Continue in this manner to cut required number of Pyramids (*Photo E*).

Garden Window

Two spectacular large-scale floral prints inspired Liz to create this quick and easy quilt. She wishes the flowers in her real garden grew as quickly as this quilt went together!

PROJECT RATING: EASY

Size: 84½" × 101½"

Blocks: 80 (7") blocks

MATERIALS

2 yards light large-scale floral print for blocks

4¼ yards medium large-scale floral print for blocks and borders

2¾ yards green print for sashing and binding

½ yard lavender print for sashing squares

Fons & Porter Quarter Inch Seam Marker (optional)

Queen-size quilt batting

7⅞ yards backing fabric

NOTE: Floral fabrics in the quilt shown are from the Dahlia Blooms collection by Kaffe Fassett and the Blue Dahlias collection by Martha Negley for Westminster Fibers.

Cutting

Measurements include ¼" seam allowances. Border strips are exact length needed. You may want to make them longer to allow for piecing variations.

From light floral print, cut:

• 8 (7⅞"-wide) strips. From strips, cut 40 (7⅞") squares.

From medium floral print, cut:

• 10 (8"-wide) strips. Piece strips to make 2 (8" × 87") side borders and 2 (8" × 85") top and bottom borders.

• 8 (7⅞"-wide) strips. From strips, cut 40 (7⅞") squares.

From green print, cut:

• 5 (7½"-wide) strips for strip sets.

• 4 (7½"-wide) strips. From strips, cut 80 (2" × 7½") sashing strips.

• 10 (2¼"-wide) strips for binding.

From lavender print, cut:

• 5 (2"-wide) strips for strip sets.

• 1 (2") sashing square.

Block Assembly

1. Referring to *Sew Easy: Quick Triangle-Squares* on page 139, join 1 light floral and 1 medium blue square to make a triangle-square. Make 80 triangle-squares.

2. Join 1 lavender print strip and 1 (7½"-wide) green print strip as shown in *Strip Set Diagram*. Make 5 strip sets. From strip sets, cut 98 (2"-wide) segments.

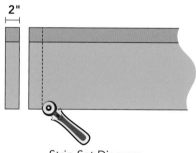

Strip Set Diagram

3. Pre-sash blocks by adding 1 green sashing strip to right edge of each block. Make 20 each of Blocks A, B, C, and D as shown in *Pre-sashing Diagrams* on page 138.

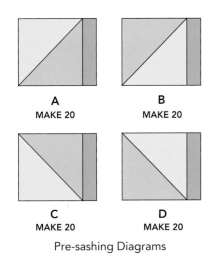

A
MAKE 20

B
MAKE 20

C
MAKE 20

D
MAKE 20

Pre-sashing Diagrams

Sew **Smart**™

As you make pre-sashed blocks, pay careful attention to the position of the light and medium triangles. —Liz

Quilt Assembly

1. Referring to *Quilt Top Assembly Diagram,* lay out 2 each of block A, B, C, and D as shown in Row 1. Join blocks to complete row. Make 3 Row 1.

2. In the same manner, make 2 Row 2, 3 Row 3, and 2 Row 4.

3. Join 8 strip set segments to make 1 sashing row as shown. Make 10 sashing rows.

4. Lay out blocks rows and sashing rows as shown in *Quilt Top Assembly Diagram;* join rows.

5. Join 10 strip set segments to form side sashing strip. Add strip to left side of quilt center. Join 8 strip set segments and lavender sashing square to form bottom sashing strip. Add strip to bottom of quilt center.

6. Add side borders to quilt center. Add top and bottom borders to quilt.

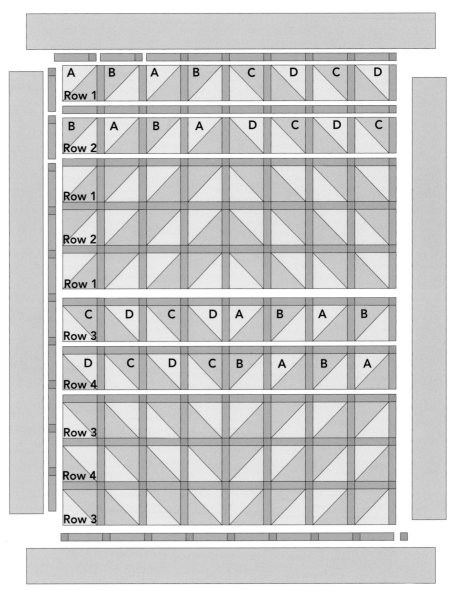

Quilt Top Assembly Diagram

Finishing

1. Divide backing fabric into 3 (2⅝-yard) lengths. Join panels lengthwise. Seams will run horizontally.

2. Layer backing, batting, and quilt top; baste. Quilt as desired. Quilt shown was machine quilted in the ditch of sashing strips and with flower designs in blocks and borders (*Quilting Diagram*).

3. Join 2¼"-wide green print strips into 1 continuous piece for straight-grain French-fold binding. Add binding to quilt.

Quilting Diagram

Quick Triangle-Squares

Our quick method for making triangle-squares begins with two squares. Use this technique to make the blocks for the *Garden Window* quilt on page 136. A Fons & Porter Quarter Inch Seam Marker offers a neat way to mark accurate sewing lines for this method.

A

1. From each of 2 fabrics, cut 1 square $7/8$" larger than the desired finished size of the triangle-square. For example, to make a triangle-square that will finish 7" as in the *Garden Window* quilt on page 136, cut $7\frac{7}{8}$" squares.

2. On the wrong side of the lighter square, place the Quarter Inch Seam Marker diagonally across the square, with the yellow center line positioned exactly at opposite corners. Mark stitching lines along both sides of the Quarter Inch Seam Marker (*Photo A*).

NOTE: If you are not using the Fons & Porter Quarter Inch Seam Marker, draw a diagonal line from corner to corner across square. Then draw sewing lines on each side of the first line, ¼" away.

3. Place lighter square atop darker square, right sides facing; stitch along both marked sewing lines.

4. Cut between rows of stitching to make 2 triangle-squares (*Photo B*). Press seam allowances toward darker fabric.

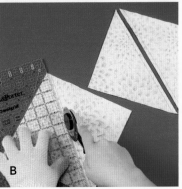

B

TRIED & TRUE

Make a stunning two-color quilt from blue-and-white prints. Fabrics shown here are from the Fleur collection by Timeless Treasures ✳

QUILT BY **Marianne Fons.**
MACHINE QUILTED BY **Jean Nolte**.

Spiderweb

Design a nostalgic nursery by incorporating 1930s reproduction fabrics. Substitute any solid color for the lavender to complement your room décor.

PROJECT RATING: INTERMEDIATE
Size: 42" × 42"
Blocks: 16 (9") Spiderweb blocks

MATERIALS

1 yard lavender solid for block corners, borders, and binding
½ yard white solid for block corners and borders
¼ yard each of 10 assorted 1930s reproduction prints for strip sets
Kaleidoscope ruler or template material
2¾ yards backing fabric
Crib-size quilt batting

Cutting

Measurements include ¼" seam allowances. Border strips are exact length needed. You may want to make them longer to allow for piecing variations. NOTE: Our Instructions call for using a 45-degree wedge or kaleidoscope ruler to cut the wedge pieces. See *Sew Easy: Using a Kaleidoscope Ruler* on page 147. If you prefer, make a template for the wedge from pattern on page 144.

From lavender solid, cut:

• 2 (4"-wide) strips. From strips, cut 16 (4") squares. Cut squares in half diagonally to make 32 half-square A triangles.

• 5 (2¼"-wide) strips for binding.

• 8 (1½"-wide) strips. From strips, cut 8 (1½" × 36½") border strips and 16 (1½") B squares.

From white solid, cut:

• 2 (4"-wide) strips. From strips, cut 16 (4") squares. Cut squares in half diagonally to make 32 half-square A triangles.

• 5 (1½"-wide) strips. From strips, cut 4 (1½" × 36½") border strips and 20 (1½") B squares.

From each reproduction print, cut:

• 5–6 strips, ranging from 1¼"–2" wide, for strip sets.

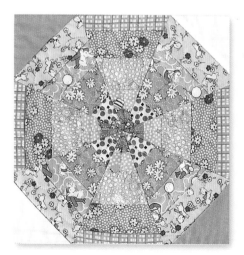

Block Assembly

1. Referring to *Strip Set Diagram*, join 4–6 strips of random color and width into a strip set 5"–5½" wide. Press seam allowances in one direction. Make 8 strip sets.

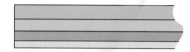

Strip Set Diagram

2. Referring to *Wedge Cutting Diagram*, use a kaleidoscope ruler or template to cut 16 wedges from each strip set. Separate the wedges into 32 sets of 4 matching pieces.

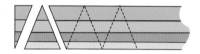

Wedge Cutting Diagram

3. Lay out 2 wedge sets as shown in *Web Assembly Diagrams*. Join wedges in pairs; join pairs to make 2 web halves. Join halves to complete 1 web.

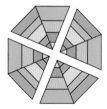 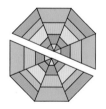

Web Assembly Diagrams

4. Referring to *Block Assembly Diagram*, add lavender A triangles to opposite corners of web. Add white A triangles to remaining corners to complete 1 block *(Block Diagram)*. Use a large ruled square to trim blocks to 9½". Make 16 Spiderweb blocks.

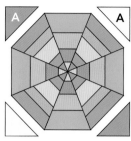

Block Assembly Diagram

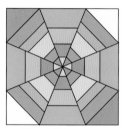

Block Diagram

Border Assembly

1. Referring to *Corner Block Assembly Diagram*, lay out 5 white B squares and 4 lavender B squares. Join into rows; join rows to complete 1 corner block *(Corner Block Diagram)*. Make 4 corner blocks.

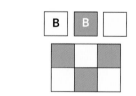

Corner Block Assembly Diagram

Corner Block Diagram

2. Referring to *Quilt Top Assembly Diagram*, join 2 lavender strips and 1 white strip to make 1 pieced border. Make 4 pieced borders.

Quilt Top Assembly Diagram

Quilt Assembly

1. Lay out blocks as shown in *Quilt Top Assembly Diagram*. Join into rows; join rows to complete quilt center.

2. Add pieced borders to 2 opposite sides of quilt center.

3. Add 1 corner block to each end of remaining pieced borders. Add borders to top and bottom of quilt.

Finishing

1. Divide backing fabric into 2 (1⅜-yard) lengths. Cut 1 piece in half

lengthwise. Join 1 narrow panel to wider panel. Press seam allowances toward narrow panel. Remaining panel is extra and can be used to make a hanging sleeve.

2. Layer backing, batting, and quilt top; baste. Quilt as desired. Quilt shown was quilted in the ditch and with a floral motif centered in each Spiderweb *(Quilting Diagram)*.

3. Join 2¼"-wide lavender strips into 1 continuous piece for straight-grain French-fold binding. Add binding to quilt.

Quilting Diagram

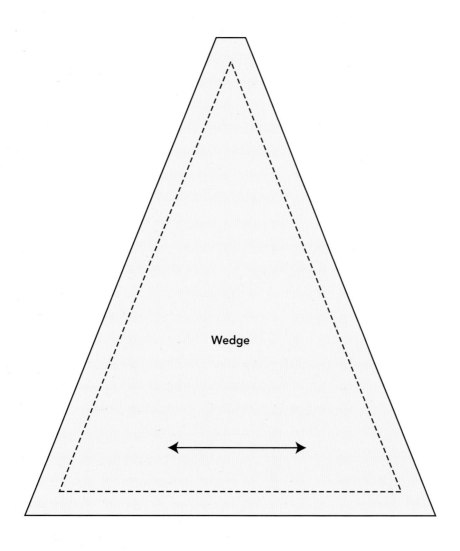

Wedge

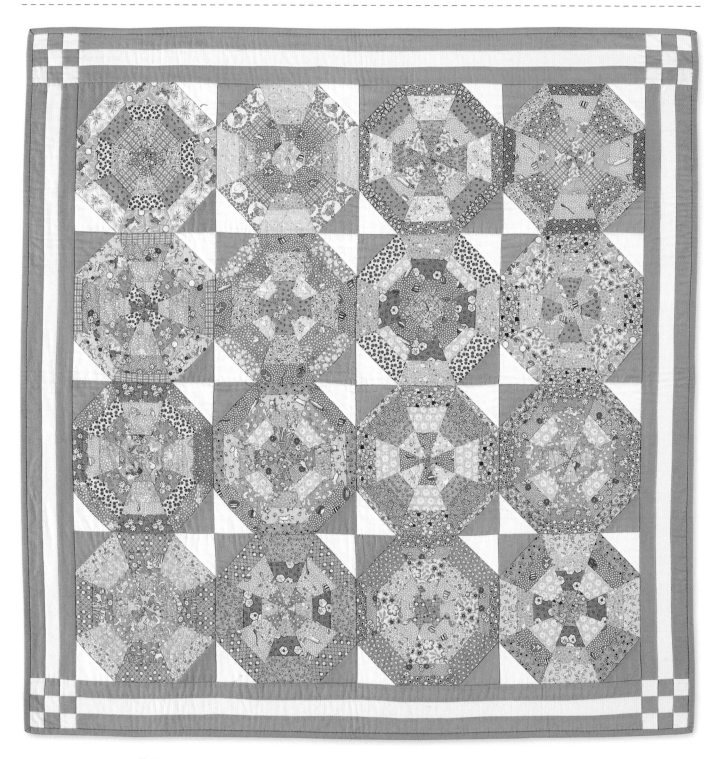

"I love the charm and freshness of 1930s-style fabrics. They tend to be busy prints, so I like to calm them down with a coordinating solid color, such as pink, yellow, green, blue, or lavender." —Marianne *

Sew Easy™

Using a Kaleidoscope Ruler

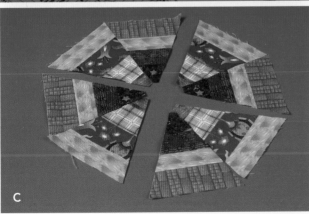

Foundation piecing scrap strips onto a wedge-shaped paper or fabric foundation is the traditional method for making Spiderweb blocks. Now, kaleidoscope rulers make short work of piecing this block.

1. Determine the size block you plan to make. If the ruler doesn't tell you the strip or strip set width needed to cut your pieces, use another ruler to measure from the line for your block size to the tip of the ruler.

2. Cut random-width strips from a variety of fabrics and join into a strip set that is the determined width or slightly wider. Press seam allowances in one direction.

3. Place line on ruler for your block size along edge of strip or strip set. Cut along both edges of ruler, trimming off end of strip set at an angle (Photo A).

4. Place strip width line on ruler along edge on opposite side of strip set. Cut along angled edge to cut 1 wedge with the opposite fabric sequence from the first wedge (Photo B).

5. To make 1 web, combine 8 wedges. We used 2 sets of 4 wedges each from different strip sets (Photo C). To complete the block, cut triangles for the block corners. Some brands of rulers include cutting lines for the corresponding corner triangles. Our instructions call for cutting triangles oversize and trimming the block to the correct size after triangles have been added.

Liz's Daisy Chain

Babies love bright colors, so make this Daisy Chain quilt for your next baby shower. Liz made her quilt in a contemporary color scheme to complement a baby's nursery.

Size: 42½" × 55¼"
Blocks: 12 (9") Daisy blocks
82 (3") Nine Patch blocks

MATERIALS

12 fat quarters★ assorted prints (2 each red, orange, green, purple, pink, and blue) for daisies and strip sets

1 fat eighth★★ yellow print for daisy centers and strip sets

2 yards white print for setting squares and block backgrounds

¾ yard green print for setting triangles and binding

Paper-backed fusible web

2¾ yards backing fabric

Crib-size quilt batting

★fat quarter = 18" × 20"

★★fat eighth = 9" × 20"

Cutting

Measurements include ¼" seam allowances. Patterns for appliqué pieces are on page 151. Follow manufacturer's instructions for using fusible web.

From each fat quarter, cut:
- 3 (1½"-wide) strips for strip sets.
- 8 Petals.

From yellow print, cut:
- 2 (1½"-wide) strips for strip sets.
- 12 Centers.

From white print, cut:
- 3 (9½"-wide) strips. From strips, cut 12 (9½") background squares.
- 5 (3½"-wide) strips. From strips, cut 48 (3½") setting squares.
- 14 (1½"-wide) strips. Cut each strip in half to make 28 (1½" x 20") strips for strip sets. One is extra.

From green print, cut:
- 2 (5½"-wide) strips. From strips, cut 11 (5½") squares and 2 (3") squares. Cut 5½" squares in half diagonally in both directions to make 44 side setting triangles. (2 are extra). Cut 3" squares in half diagonally to make 4 corner setting triangles.
- 6 (2¼"-wide) strips for binding.

Block Assembly

1. Referring to *Daisy Block Diagram*, center 8 Petals and 1 Center atop 1 white background square; fuse in place. Machine appliqué using matching thread to complete 1 Daisy block. Make 12 Daisy blocks.

Daisy Block Diagram

2. Join 2 print strips and 1 white strip as shown in *Strip Set A Diagam*. Press seam allowances toward dark strips. Make 13 Strip Set A. From strip sets, cut 164 (1½"-wide) A segments.

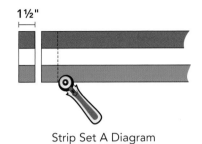

1½"

Strip Set A Diagram

3. Join 2 white strips and 1 print strip as shown in *Strip Set B Diagam*. Press seam allowances toward dark strip. Make 7 Strip Set B. From strip sets, cut 82 (1½"-wide) B segments.

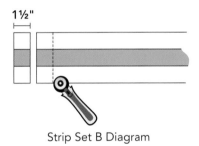

1½"

Strip Set B Diagram

4. Referring to *Nine Patch Unit Diagrams*, join 1 B and 2 A segments to make 1 Nine Patch Unit. Make 82 Nine Patch Units.

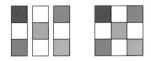

Nine Patch Unit Diagrams

5. Referring to *Double Nine Patch Block Diagrams*, join 5 Nine Patch Units and 4 setting squares to make 1 Double Nine Patch block. Make 6 Double Nine Patch blocks.

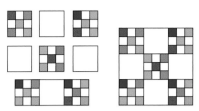

Double Nine Patch Block Diagrams

Setting Triangle Assembly

1. Lay out 4 Nine Patch Units, 2 white setting squares, and 2 green print side setting triangles as shown in *Side Setting Unit Diagrams*. Join to make 1 Side Setting Unit. Make 10 Side Setting Units.

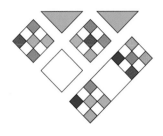

Side Setting Unit Diagrams

2. Lay out 3 Nine Patch Units, 1 white setting square, 2 green print side setting triangles, and 1 green print corner setting triangle as shown in *Corner Setting Unit Diagrams*. Join to make 1 Corner Setting Unit. Make 4 Corner Setting Units.

Corner Setting Unit Diagrams

Quilt Assembly

1. Lay out Daisy blocks, Double Nine Patch blocks, Side Setting Units, Corner Setting Units, and remaining green print setting triangles as shown in *Quilt Top Assembly Diagram*.

2. Add green print setting triangles to setting units.

3. Join into diagonal rows; join rows to complete quilt top.

Quilting and Finishing

1. Divide backing fabric into 2 (1⅜-yard) lengths. Cut 1 piece in half lengthwise. Sew 1 narrow panel to wider panel. Seam will run horizontally. Remaining panel is extra and can be used to make a hanging sleeve.

2. Layer backing, batting, and quilt top; baste. Quilt as desired. Quilt shown was outline quilted around daisies and in the ditch around blocks.

3. Join 2¼"-wide green print strips into 1 continuous piece for straight-grain French-fold binding. Add binding to quilt. ✳

Quilt Top Assembly Diagram

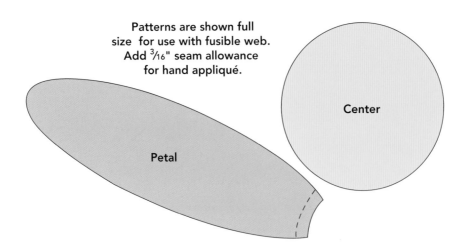

Patterns are shown full size for use with fusible web. Add ³⁄₁₆" seam allowance for hand appliqué.

Petal

Center

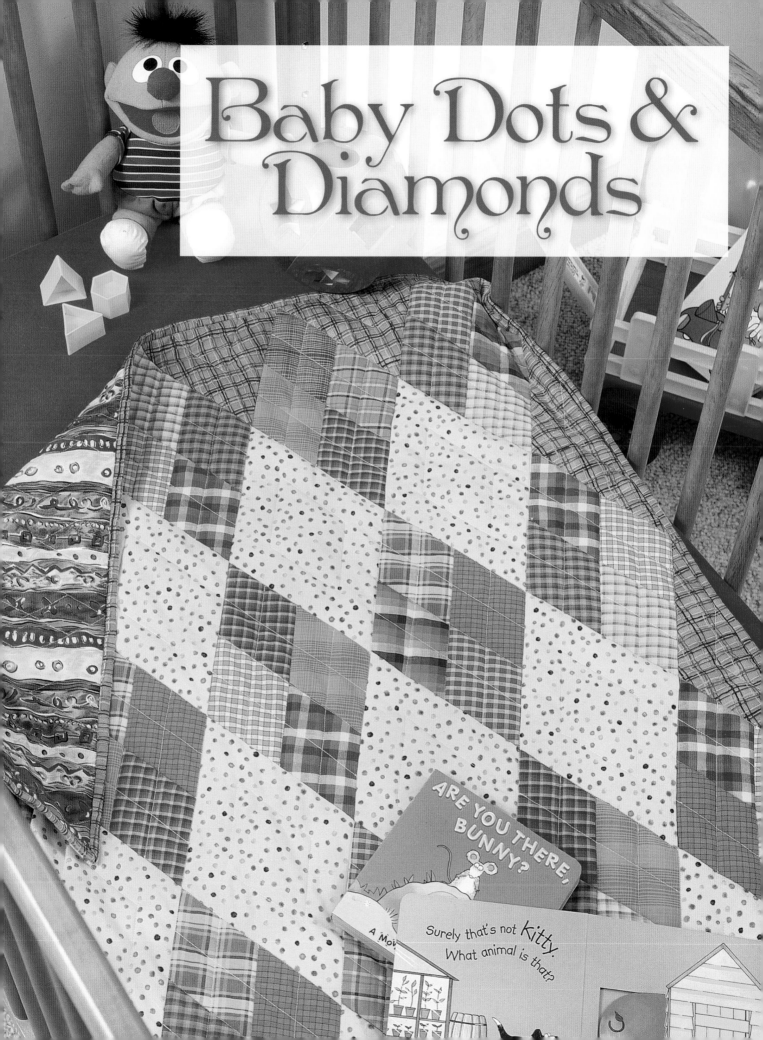

Baby Dots & Diamonds

If you have avoided diamond shapes in quilts because you thought they were too difficult, this is the perfect project for giving them a try. This quilt is fun to make because there are no set-in pieces.

PROJECT RATING: INTERMEDIATE
Size: 37½" × 44"
Blocks: 24 Diamond Four Patch blocks

MATERIALS

- 6 fat eighths★ assorted blue plaids for strip sets
- 6 fat eighths★ assorted orange plaids for strip sets
- ⅝ yard yellow print fabric for setting diamonds
- 1 yard turquoise plaid for border triangles and binding
- 1⅜ yards backing fabric
- Crib-size quilt batting
- ★fat eighth = 9" × 20"

Cutting

Measurements include ¼" seam allowances. Refer to *Sew Easy: Rotary Cutting Angles* on page 154 to cut diamonds and setting triangles.

From each plaid fat eighth, cut:
- 2 (3¼"-wide) strips for strip sets.

From yellow print, cut:
- 3 (6"-wide) strips. From strips, cut 15 (6") diamonds.

From turquoise plaid, cut:
- 2 (6¼"-wide) strips. From strips, cut 14 top and bottom setting triangles.
- 2 (3¾"-wide) strips. From strips, cut 6 side setting triangles.
- 5 (2¼"-wide) strips for binding.

Block Assembly

1. Join 2 plaid (3¼"-wide) strips, offsetting them by 1½" as shown in *Strip Set Diagram*. Make 12 strip sets.

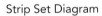

Strip Set Diagram

2. Referring to *Sew Easy: Making Pieced Diamond Units* on page 155, cut 48 strip set segments.
3. Join 2 segments to make 1 Diamond Four Patch block *(Block Diagram)*. Make 24 blocks.

Block Diagram

Quilt Assembly

1. Lay out Diamond Four Patch blocks, yellow print setting diamonds, and border setting triangles as shown in *Quilt Top Assembly Diagram*.
2. Join into diagonal rows; join rows to complete quilt center.
3. Trim border corner triangles even with sides of quilt.

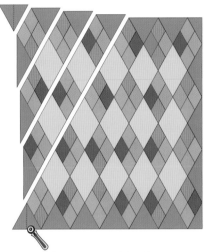

Quilt Top Assembly Diagram

Finishing

1. Layer backing, batting, and quilt top; baste. Quilt as desired. Quilt shown has a diamond grid in the Four Patch blocks, diamonds in the yellow setting blocks, and half diamonds in the border triangles.
2. Join 2¼"-wide turquoise plaid strips into 1 continuous piece for straight-grain French-fold binding. Add binding to quilt. ✳

Rotary Cutting Angles

Diamonds and setting triangles are easy to cut with a rotary cutter and a ruler that has 60-degree and 30-degree angle markings. The strip measurements given here are for *Baby Dots & Diamonds*, but they may be adapted for other sizes of diamonds and triangles.

Cutting Large Diamonds

1. Cut strip 6" wide.
2. Using regular ruler, trim end of strip at 60-degree angle *(Photo A)*.
3. Position 6" line on ruler on the angled edge. Cut along edge of ruler to make 1 diamond. Continue in this manner to cut desired number of diamonds *(Photo B)*.

Cutting Top and Bottom Setting Triangles

1. To cut top and bottom setting triangles, place 60-degree line on ruler across top of 6¼"-wide strip and cut along edge of ruler *(Photo C)*.
2. Place other 60-degree line on ruler across bottom of strip and cut triangle *(Photo D)*.

Cutting Side Setting Triangles

1. To cut side setting triangles, place 30-degree line on ruler across top of 3¾"-wide strip and cut along edge of ruler *(Photo E)*.
2. Place other 30-degree line on ruler across bottom of strip and cut triangle *(Photo F)*.

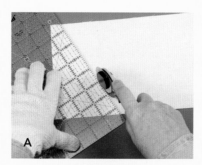
A

B

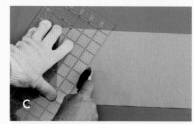
C

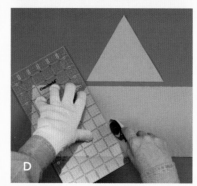
D

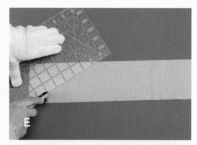
E

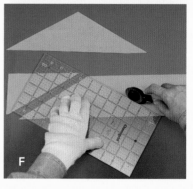
F

Sew **Smart**™

Rotary cutting diamonds is a bit tricky. I like to check them for accuracy by folding them in half either vertically or horizontally from point to point. Because a diamond is symmetrical, the raw edges and points should meet when they are folded.
—Marianne

Making Pieced Diamond Units

Follow our easy instructions for making diamond units from strip sets.

Making Pieced Diamonds

1. Cut strips 3¼" wide. Make a strip set by joining 2 strips, offsetting them at 1 end by about 1½". Trim end of strip set at 60-degree angle.

2. Position 3¼" line of ruler on angled cut edge and cut along edge of ruler (*Photo A*). Continue in this manner to cut desired number of segments.

3. Lay out 2 segments as shown in *Photo B*. Join segments to make pieced diamond, matching diamond seams ¼" from raw edge as shown in *Photo C*. Seams form an "X" at seam line.

4. If seams do not match after they are stitched, give them the "pinch test" by pinching a slightly deeper seam with your fingers. If the alignment becomes worse (*Photo D*), your seam was too wide. You will need to pick out the part of the seam where diamonds meet and restitch with a slightly narrower seam. If the alignment improves with pinching, restitch with a slightly wider seam at diamond intersection.

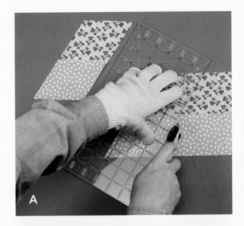

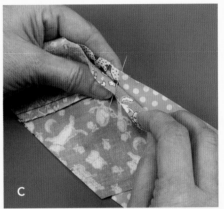

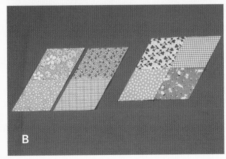

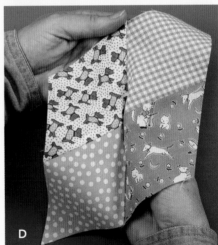

Not Rocket Science

Marianne made this quilt when she and Liz were experimenting with string piecing techniques for a retreat. The name came about because the technique for making the quilt was easy, and the shapes in the block reminded Marianne of bottle rockets.

Finished Size: 42" × 54"
Blocks: 48 (6") blocks

MATERIALS

1¼ yards blue print for blocks and binding

¾ yard white print for blocks

17 fat eighths★ assorted bright prints for blocks and borders

3 yards backing

Crib-size batting

★fat eighth = 9" × 20"

Cutting

Measurements include ¼" seam allowances. Border strips are exact length needed. You may want to make them longer to allow for piecing variations.

From blue print, cut:

• 3 (4¾"-wide) strips. From strips, cut 24 (4¾") squares. Cut squares in half diagonally to make 48 half-square A triangles.

• 2 (3"-wide) strips. From strips, cut 24 (3") squares. Cut squares in half diagonally to make 48 half-square B triangles.

• 6 (2¼"-wide) strips for binding.

From white print, cut:

• 3 (4¾"-wide) strips. From strips, cut 24 (4¾") squares. Cut squares in half diagonally to make 48 half-square A triangles.

• 2 (3"-wide) strips. From strips, cut 24 (3") squares. Cut squares in half diagonally to make 48 half-square B triangles.

From each fat eighth, cut:

• 4 assorted-width strips ranging from 1½"–3" wide.

Block Assembly

1. Referring to *Strip Set Diagram*, join strips cut from fat eighths randomly by color and width into 17 strip sets at least 6¼" wide.

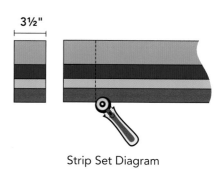

Strip Set Diagram

2. Trim 10 strip sets to 6" wide. From these, cut 48 (3½" × 6") segments.

3. Lay out 1 segment, 2 blue print A triangles, and 2 white print B triangles as shown in *Block Assembly Diagram*. Join to complete 1 block *(Block Diagram)*. Make 24 blocks.

Block Assembly Diagram

Block Diagram

4. In the same manner, make 24 blocks using 1 strip set segment, 2 white print A triangles, and 2 blue print B triangles in each.

Border Assembly

1. From remaining strip sets, cut 32 (3½"-wide) segments.

2. Join segments end to end to make 1 long strip. From long strip, cut 2 (3½" × 48½") side borders, 2 (3½" × 36½") top and bottom borders, and 4 (3½") squares for border corners.

Quilt Assembly

1. Lay out blocks as shown in *Quilt Top Assembly Diagram*. Join into rows; join rows to complete quilt center.

2. Add pieced side borders to quilt center. Add 1 corner square to each end of top and bottom pieced borders. Add borders to top and bottom of quilt.

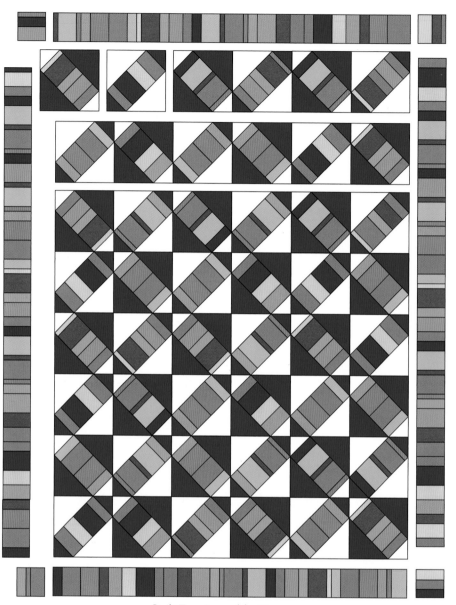

Quilt Top Assembly Diagram

Quilting and Finishing

1. Divide backing fabric into 2 (1½-yard) lengths. Cut 1 piece in half lengthwise to make 2 narrow panels. Join 1 narrow panel to wider panel. Press seam allowance toward narrow panel. Seam will run horizontally. Remaining panel is extra and can be used to make a hanging sleeve.

2. Layer backing, batting, and quilt top; baste. Quilt as desired. Quilt shown was quilted with concentric squares and spirals.

3. Join 2¼"-wide blue print strips into 1 continuous piece for straight-grain French-fold binding. Add binding to quilt. ✳

General Instructions

Basic Supplies

You'll need a **sewing machine (A)** in good working order to construct patchwork blocks, join blocks together, add borders, and machine quilt. We encourage you to purchase a machine from a local dealer, who can help you with service in the future, rather than from a discount store. Another option may be to borrow a machine from a friend or family member. If the machine has not been used in a while, have it serviced by a local dealer to make sure it is in good working order. If you need an extension cord, one with a surge protector is a good idea.

A **rotary cutting mat (B)** is essential for accurate and safe rotary cutting. Purchase one that is no smaller than 18" × 24".

Rotary cutting mats are made of "self-healing" material that can be used over and over.

A **rotary cutter (C)** is a cutting tool that looks like a pizza cutter, and has a very sharp blade. We recommend starting with a standard size 45mm rotary cutter. Always lock or close your cutter when it is not in use, and keep it out of the reach of children.

A **safety glove** (also known as a *Klutz Glove)* **(D)** is also recommended. Wear your safety glove on the hand that is holding the ruler in place. Because it is made of cut-resistant material, the safety glove protects your non-cutting hand from accidents that can occur if your cutting hand slips while cutting.

An acrylic **ruler (E)** is used in combination with your cutting mat and rotary cutter. We recommend the Fons & Porter

8" × 14" ruler, but a 6" × 12" ruler is another good option. You'll need a ruler with inch, quarter-inch, and eighth-inch markings that show clearly for ease of measuring. Choose a ruler with 45-degree-angle, 30-degree-angle, and 60-degree-angle lines marked on it as well.

Since you will be using 100% cotton fabric for your quilts, use **cotton or cotton-covered polyester thread (F)** for piecing and quilting. Avoid 100% polyester thread, as it tends to snarl.

Keep a pair of small **scissors (G)** near your sewing machine for cutting threads.

Thin, good quality **straight pins (H)** are preferred by quilters. The pins included with pin cushions are normally too thick to use for piecing, so discard them. Purchase a box of nickel-plated brass **safety pins** size #1 **(I)** to use for pin-basting the layers of your quilt together for machine quilting.

Invest in a 120"-long dressmaker's **measuring tape (J)**. This will come in handy when making borders for your quilt.

A 0.7–0.9mm mechanical **pencil (K)** works well for marking on your fabric.

Invest in a quality sharp **seam ripper (L)**. Every quilter gets well-acquainted with her seam ripper!

Set up an **ironing board (M)** and **iron (N)** in your sewing area. Pressing yardage before cutting, and pressing patchwork seams as you go are both essential for quality quiltmaking. Select an iron that has steam capability.

Masking **tape (O)** or painter's tape works well to mark your sewing machine so you can sew an accurate ¼" seam. You will also use tape to hold your backing fabric taut as you prepare your quilt sandwich for machine quilting.

The most exciting item that you will need for quilting is **fabric (P)**. Quilters generally prefer 100% cotton fabrics for their quilts. This fabric is woven from cotton threads, and has a lengthwise and a crosswise grain. The term "bias" is used to describe the diagonal grain of the fabric. If you make a 45-degree angle cut through a square of cotton fabric, the cut edges will be bias edges, which are quite stretchy. As you learn more quiltmaking techniques, you'll learn how bias can work to your advantage or disadvantage.

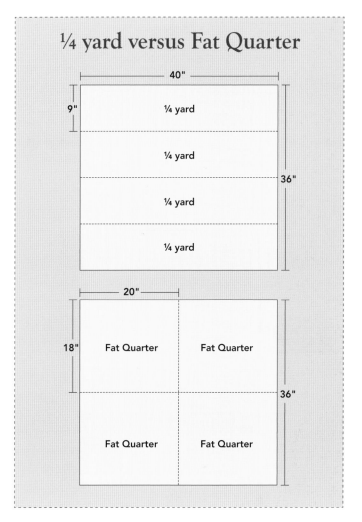

¼ yard versus Fat Quarter

Fabric is sold by the yard at quilt shops and fabric stores. Quilting fabric is generally about 40"–44" wide, so a yard is about 40" wide by 36" long. As you collect fabrics to build your own personal stash, you will buy yards, half yards (about 18" × 40"), quarter yards (about 9" × 40"), as well as other lengths.

Many quilt shops sell "fat quarters," a special cut favored by quilters. A fat quarter is created by cutting a half yard down the fold line into two 18" × 20" pieces (fat quarters) that are sold separately. Quilters like the nearly square shape of the fat quarter because it is more useful than the narrow regular quarter yard cut.

Batting (Q) is the filler between quilt top and backing that makes your quilt a quilt. It can be cotton, polyester, cotton-polyester blend, wool, silk, or other natural materials, such as bamboo or corn. Make sure the batting you buy is at least six inches wider and six inches longer than your quilt top.

Accurate Cutting

Measuring and cutting accuracy are important for successful quilting. Measure at least twice, and cut once!

Cut strips across the fabric width unless directed otherwise.

Cutting for patchwork usually begins with cutting strips, which are then cut into smaller pieces. First, cut straight strips from a fat quarter:

1. Fold fat quarter in half with selvedge edge at the top (*Photo A*).

2. Straighten edge of fabric by placing ruler atop fabric, aligning one of the lines on ruler with selvedge edge of fabric (*Photo B*). Cut along right edge of ruler.

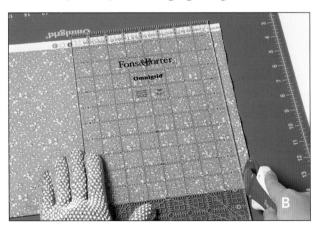

3. Rotate fabric, and use ruler to measure from cut edge to desired strip width (*Photo C*). Measurements in instructions include ¼" seam allowances.

4. After cutting the required number of strips, cut strips into squares and label them.

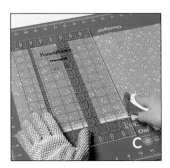

Setting up Your Sewing Machine

Sew Accurate ¼" Seams

Standard seam width for patchwork and quiltmaking is ¼". Some machines come with a patchwork presser foot, also known as a quarter-inch foot. If your machine doesn't have a quarter-inch foot, you may be able to purchase one from a dealer. Or, you can create a quarter-inch seam guide on your machine using masking tape or painter's tape.

Place an acrylic ruler on your sewing machine bed under the presser foot. Slowly turn handwheel until the tip of the needle barely rests atop the ruler's quarter-inch mark (*Photo A*). Make sure the lines on the ruler are parallel to the lines on the machine throat plate. Place tape on the machine bed along edge of ruler (*Photo B*).

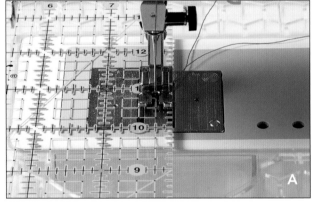

Take a Simple Seam Test

Seam accuracy is critical to machine piecing, so take this simple test once you have your quarter-inch presser foot on your machine or have created a tape guide.

Place 2 (2½") squares right sides together, and sew with a scant ¼" seam. Open squares and finger press seam. To finger press, with right sides facing you, press the seam to one side with your fingernail. Measure across pieces, raw edge to raw edge (*Photo C*). If they measure 4½", you have passed the test! Repeat the test as needed to make sure you can confidently sew a perfect ¼" seam.

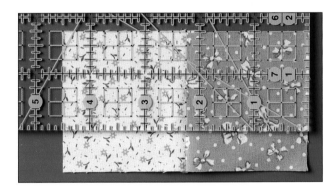

Sewing Comfortably

Other elements that promote pleasant sewing are good lighting, a comfortable chair, background music—and chocolate! Good lighting promotes accurate sewing. The better you can see what you are working on, the better your results. A comfortable chair enables you to sew for longer periods of time. An office chair with a good back rest and adjustable height works well. Music helps keep you relaxed. Chocolate is, for many quilters, simply a necessity.

Tips for Patchwork and Pressing

As you sew more patchwork, you'll develop your own shortcuts and favorite methods. Here are a few favored by many quilters:

● As you join patchwork units to form rows, and join rows to form blocks, press seams in opposite directions from row to row whenever possible (*Photo A*). By pressing seams one direction in the first row and the opposite direction in the next row, you will often create seam allowances that abut when rows are joined (*Photo B*). Abutting or nesting seams are ideal for forming perfectly matched corners on the right side of your quilt blocks and quilt top. Such pressing is not always possible, so don't worry if you end up with seam allowances facing the same direction as you join units.

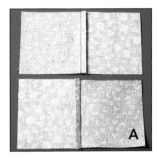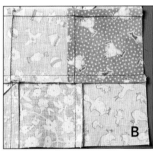

● Sew on and off a small, folded fabric square to prevent bobbin thread from bunching at throat plate (*Photo C*). You'll also save thread, which means fewer stops to wind bobbins, and fewer hanging threads to be snipped. Repeated use of the small piece of fabric gives it lots of thread "legs," so some quilters call it a spider.

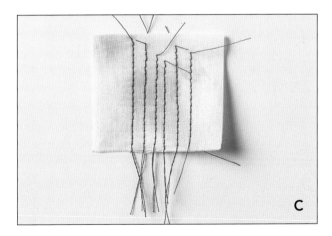

- Chain piece patchwork to reduce the amount of thread you use, and minimize the number and length of threads you need to trim from patchwork. Without cutting threads at the end of a seam, take 3–4 stitches without any fabric under the needle, creating a short thread chain approximately ⅛" long (*Photo D*). Repeat until you have a long line of pieces. Remove chain from machine, clip threads between units, and press seams.

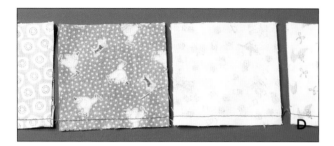

- Trim off tiny triangle tips (sometimes called dog ears) created when making triangle-square units (*Photo E*). Trimming triangles reduces bulk and makes patchwork units and blocks lie flatter. Though no one will see the back of your quilt top once it's quilted, a neat back free of dangling threads and patchwork points is the mark of a good quilter. Also, a smooth, flat quilt top is easier to quilt, whether by hand or machine.

- Careful pressing will make your patchwork neat and crisp, and will help make your finished quilt top lie flat. Ironing and pressing are two different skills. Iron fabric to remove wrinkles using a back and forth, smoothing motion. Press patchwork and quilt blocks by raising and gently lowering the iron atop your work. After sewing a patchwork unit, first press the seam with the unit closed, pressing to set, or embed, the stitching. Setting the seam this way will help produce straight, crisp seams. Open the unit and press on the right side with the seam toward the darkest fabric,

being careful to not form a pleat in your seam, and carefully pressing the patchwork flat.

- Many quilters use finger pressing to open and flatten seams of small units before pressing with an iron. To finger press, open patchwork unit with right side of fabric facing you. Run your fingernail firmly along seam, making sure unit is fully open with no pleat.

- Careful use of steam in your iron will make seams and blocks crisp and flat (*Photo F*). Aggressive ironing can stretch blocks out of shape, and is a common pitfall for new quilters.

Adding Borders

Follow these simple instructions to make borders that fit perfectly on your quilt.

1. Find the length of your quilt by measuring through the quilt center, not along the edges, since the edges may have stretched. Take 3 measurements and average them to determine the length to cut your side borders (*Diagram A*). Cut 2 side borders this length.

2. Fold border strips in half to find center. Pinch to create crease mark or place a pin at center. Fold quilt top in half crosswise to find center of side. Attach side borders to quilt center by pinning them at the ends and the center, and easing in any fullness. If quilt edge is a bit longer than border, pin and sew with border on top; if border is

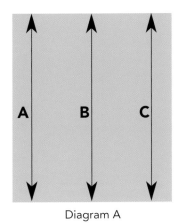

Diagram A

A _____

B _____

C _____

TOTAL _____

_____ ÷3

AVERAGE
LENGTH _____

HELPFUL TIP

Use the following decimal conversions to calculate
your quilt's measurements:

⅛" = .125   ⅝" = .625
¼" = .25   ¾" = .75
⅜" = .375   ⅞" = .875
½" = .5

slightly longer than quilt top, pin and sew with border on
the bottom. Machine feed dogs will ease in the fullness of
the longer piece. Press seams toward borders.

3. Find the width of your quilt by measuring across the
quilt and side borders (*Diagram B*). Take 3 measurements
and average them to determine the length to cut your
top and bottom borders. Cut 2 borders this length.

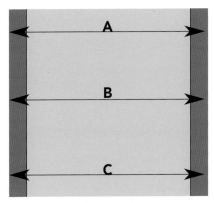

Diagram B

4. Mark centers of borders and top and bottom edges
of quilt top. Attach top and bottom borders to quilt,
pinnning at ends and center, and easing in any fullness
(*Diagram C*). Press seams toward borders.

Diagram C

5. Gently steam press entire quilt top on one side and then
the other. When pressing on wrong side, trim off any
loose threads.

Joining Border Strips

Not all quilts have borders, but they are a nice complement to
a quilt top. If your border is longer than 40", you will need
to join 2 or more strips to make a border the required length.
You can join border strips with either a straight seam parallel
to the ends of the strips (*Photo A* on page 166), or with a
diagonal seam. For the diagonal seam method, place one
border strip perpendicular to another strip, rights sides facing
(*Photo B*). Stitch diagonally across strips as shown. Trim seam
allowance to ¼". Press seam open (*Photo C*).

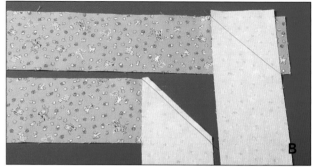

Quilting Your Quilt

Quilters today joke that there are three ways to quilt a quilt—by hand, by machine, or by check. Some enjoy making quilt tops so much, they prefer to hire a professional machine quilter to finish their work. The Split Nine Patch baby quilt shown at left has simple machine quilting that you can do yourself.

Decide what color thread will look best on your quilt top before choosing your backing fabric. A thread color that will blend in with the quilt top is a good choice for beginners. Choose backing fabric that will blend with your thread as well. A print fabric is a good choice for hiding less-than-perfect machine quilting. The backing fabric must be at least 3"–4" larger than your quilt top on all 4 sides. For example: if your quilt top measures 44" × 44", your backing needs to be at least 50" × 50". If your quilt top is 80" × 96", then your backing fabric needs to be at least 86" × 102".

For quilt tops 36" wide or less, use a single width of fabric for the backing. Buy enough length to allow adequate margin at quilt edges, as noted above. When your quilt is wider than 36", one option is to use 60"-, 90"-, or 108"-wide fabric for the quilt backing. Because fabric selection is limited for wide fabrics, quilters generally piece the quilt backing from 44/45"-wide fabric. Plan on 40"–42" of usable fabric width when estimating how much fabric to purchase. Plan your piecing strategy to avoid having a seam along the veritcal or horizontal center of the quilt.

For a quilt 37"–60" wide, a backing with horizontal seams is usually the most economical use of fabric. For example, for a quilt 50" × 70", vertical seams would require 152", or 4¼ yards, of 44/45"-wide fabric (76" + 76" = 152"). Horizontal seams would require 112", or 3¼ yards (56" + 56" = 112").

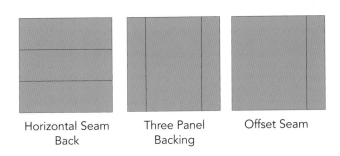

Horizontal Seam Back

Three Panel Backing

Offset Seam

For a quilt 61"–80" wide, most quilters piece a three-panel backing, with vertical seams, from two lengths of fabric. Cut one of the pieces in half lengthwise, and sew the halves to opposite sides of the wider panel. Press the seams away from the center panel.

For a quilt 81"–120" wide, you will need three lengths of fabric, plus extra margin. For example, for a quilt 108" × 108", purchase at least 342", or 9½ yards, of 44/45"-wide fabric (114" + 114" + 114" = 342").

For a three-panel backing, pin the selvage edge of the enter panel to the selvage edge of the side panel, with edges aligned and right sides facing. Machine stitch with a ½" seam. Trim seam allowances to ¼", trimming off the selvages from both panels at once. Press the seam away from the center of the quilt. Repeat on other side of center panel.

For a two-panel backing, join panels in the same manner as above, and press the seam to one side.

Create a "quilt sandwich" by layering your backing, batting, and quilt top. Find the crosswise center of the backing fabric by folding it in half. Mark with a pin on each side. Lay backing down on a table or floor, wrong side up. Tape corners and edges of backing to the surface with masking or painter's tape so that backing is taut (*Photo A*).

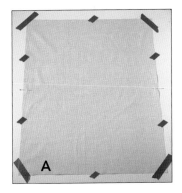

A

Fold batting in half crosswise and position it atop backing fabric, centering folded edge at center of backing (*Photo B*). Unfold batting and smooth it out atop backing (*Photo C*).

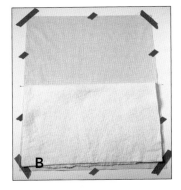

B

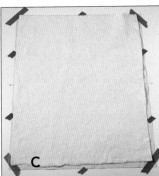

C

In the same manner, fold the quilt top in half crosswise and center it atop backing and batting (*Photo D*). Unfold top and smooth it out atop batting (*Photo E*).

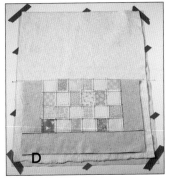

D

E

Use safety pins to pin baste the layers (*Photo F*). Pins should be about a fist width apart. A special tool, called a Kwik Klip, or a grapefruit spoon makes closing the pins easier. As you slide a pin through all three layers, slide the point of the pin into one of the tool's grooves. Push on the tool to help close the pin.

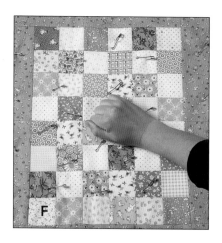

For straight line quilting, install an even feed or walking foot on your machine. This presser foot helps all three layers of your quilt move through the machine evenly without bunching.

Walking Foot   Stitching "in the ditch"

An easy way to quilt your first quilt is to stitch "in the ditch" along seam lines. No marking is needed for this type of quilting.

Binding Your Quilt

Preparing Binding

Strips for quilt binding may be cut either on the straight of grain or on the bias. For the quilts in this booklet, cut strips on the straight of grain.

1. Measure the perimeter of your quilt and add approximately 24" to allow for mitered corners and finished ends.
2. Cut the number of strips necessary to achieve desired length. We like to cut binding strips 2¼" wide.
3. Join your strips with diagonal seams into 1 continuous piece (*Photo A*). Press the seams open. (See page 165 for instructions for the diagonal seams method of joining strips.)

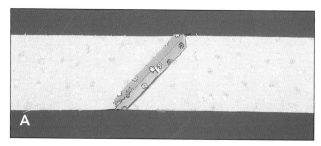

4. Press your binding in half lengthwise, with wrong sides facing, to make French-fold binding (*Photo B*).

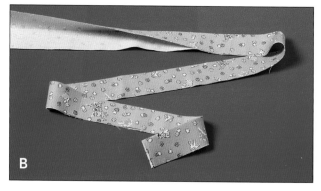

Attaching Binding

Attach the binding to your quilt using an even-feed or walking foot. This prevents puckering when sewing through the three layers.

1. Choose beginning point along one side of quilt. Do not start at a corner. Match the two raw edges of the binding strip to the raw edge of the quilt top. The folded edge

will be free and to left of seam line (*Photo C*). Leave 12" or longer tail of binding strip dangling free from beginning point. Stitch, using ¼" seam, through all layers.

2. For mitered corners, stop stitching ¼" from corner; backstitch, and remove quilt from sewing machine (*Photo D*). Place a pin ¼" from corner to mark where you will stop stitching.

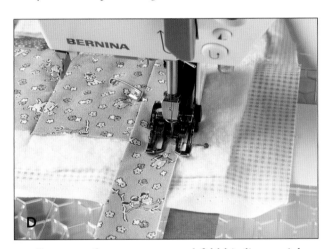

Rotate quilt quarter turn and fold binding straight up, away from corner, forming 45-degree-angle fold (*Photo E*).

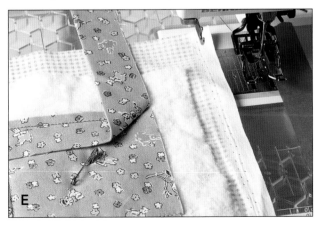

Bring binding straight down in line with next edge to be sewn, leaving top fold even with raw edge of previously sewn side (*Photo F*). Begin stitching at top edge, sewing through all layers (*Photo G*).

3. To finish binding, stop stitching about 8" away from starting point, leaving about a 12" tail at end (*Photo H*). Bring beginning and end of binding to center of 8" opening and fold each back, leaving about ¼" space

between the two folds of binding (*Photo I*). (Allowing this ¼" extra space is critical, as binding tends to stretch when it is stitched to the quilt. If the folded ends meet at this point, your binding will be too long for the space after the ends are joined.) Crease folds of binding with your fingernail.

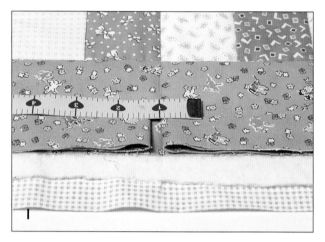

4. Open out each edge of binding and draw line across wrong side of binding on creased fold line, as shown in *Photo J*. Draw line along lengthwise fold of binding at same spot to create an X (*Photo K*).

5. With edge of ruler at marked X, line up 45-degree-angle marking on ruler with one long side of binding (*Photo L*). Draw diagonal line across binding as shown in *Photo M*.

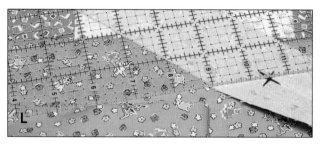

Repeat for other end of binding. Lines must angle in same direction (*Photo N*).

6. Pin binding ends together with right sides facing, pin-matching diagonal lines as shown in *Photo O*. Binding ends will be at right angles to each other. Machine-stitch along diagonal line, removing pins as you stitch (*Photo P*).

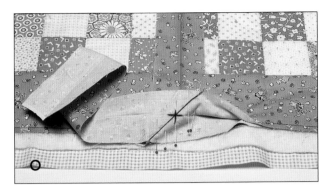

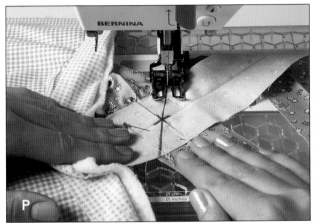

8. Finger press diagonal seam open (*Photo S*). Fold binding in half and finish stitching binding to quilt (*Photo T*).

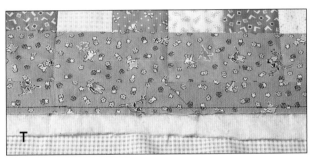

7. Lay binding against quilt to double-check that it is correct length (*Photo Q*). Trim ends of binding ¼" from diagonal seam (*Photo R*).

Hand Stitching Binding to Quilt Back

1. Trim any excess batting and quilt back with scissors or a rotary cutter (*Photo A*). Leave enough batting (about ⅛" beyond quilt top) to fill binding uniformly when it is turned to quilt back.

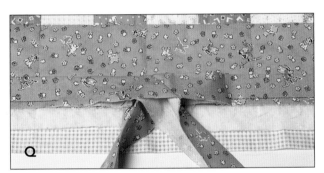

- -

2. Bring folded edge of binding to quilt back so that it covers machine stitching. Blindstitch folded edge to quilt backing, using a few pins just ahead of stitching to hold binding in place (*Photo B*).

3. Continue stitching to corner. Fold unstitched binding from next side under, forming a 45-degree angle and a mitered corner. Stitch mitered folds on both front and back (*Photo C*).

Finishing Touches

- **Label your quilt so the recipient and future generations know who made it.** To make a label, use a fabric marking pen to write the details on a small piece of solid color fabric (*Photo A*). To make writing easier, put pieces of masking tape on the wrong side. Remove tape after writing. Use your iron to turn under ¼" on each edge, then stitch the label to the back of your quilt using a blindstitch, taking care not to sew through to quilt top.

- **Take a photo of your quilt.** Keep your photos in an album or journal along with notes, fabric swatches, and other information about the quilts.
- **If your quilt is a gift, include care instructions.** Some quilt shops carry pre-printed care labels you can sew onto the quilt (*Photo B*). Or, make a care label using the method described above.

Quilting the Quilt
Fine Feathers

BY **Marianne Fons**

The beautiful feathered quilting designs admired on classic Amish and other antique quilts are the *crème de la crème* of quilting motifs. With a little practice, you can draw them yourself.

I still remember the day I saw a feather circle for the first time. Liz Porter and I had traveled to a quilt show near Ames, Iowa—quite an undertaking for us in 1977, when we were mothers with young children. We thought that feather circle was the most beautiful quilting design we had ever seen.

After that, we tried to put feathers on our own early quilts, but were frustrated because the patterns in books and the stencils we bought were never the right size. Eventually, we started experimenting with feathers ourselves and found out you don't have to be Amish or an artist to draw and quilt feathers. Over the next few years, we developed techniques that work every time and began teaching our methods to students in our classes for quilt guilds, shops, and at quilt conferences.

I wrote *Fine Feathers, A Quilter's Guide to Customizing Traditional Feather Quilting Designs* in 1988. I dedicated it to Liz, who was working as a quilt book editor at Meredith Corporation at the time. Published by C & T Publishing, *Fine Feathers* was designed as a workbook to use to teach yourself to customize all types of feather quilting designs—straight and undulating plumes, borders, circles, "fancies," and, ultimately, the designs you'd need for a whole cloth quilt.

I'd like to give you a brief lesson in drawing feathers yourself. You'll do a few exercises to learn the fundamentals of feather construction. After you draw some lines of straight feathers and some curving ones, I'll show you how to draw the most beloved quilting design of all time, the feather circle, any size you want.

Don't be afraid to try—Liz and I have shared these techniques and more with thousands of students with 100% success!

Sew Smart™

When drawing feathers, use a mechanical pencil and a good eraser. This kind of pencil keeps a nice point. Erase often and keep sketching to develop your skills.

When you draw a feather, "sketch" it by extending the pencil line little by little instead of drawing it in a single motion. —Marianne

Basic Feathering

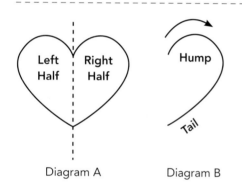

Diagram A   Diagram B

A valentine heart is a familiar shape that anyone can draw. Feather designs are made up of simple half hearts positioned on opposite sides of a center line, or vein *(Diagram A)*. On one side of the vein you have left-hand sides of hearts, on the other, right-hand sides of hearts. The single, half hearts that make up feather designs have a "hump" and a "tail" *(Diagram B)*.

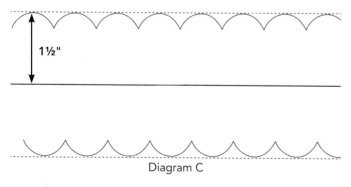

Diagram C

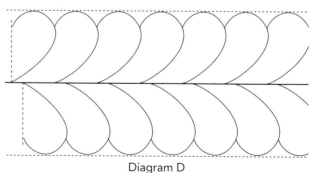

Diagram D

Straight Feathers On a piece of paper, draw a straight line about 3" from the top edge of the paper to make a center vein. Draw outer guidelines 1½" to each side of the center vein. Use a quarter to draw helping scallops just inside the outer guidelines on each side *(Diagram C)*. Draw nice, even half circles. Offset the half circles slightly on opposite sides so the tails of your feathers won't meet at the middle. Draw right-hand sides of hearts on one side of the center vein and left-hand sides of hearts on the other side as shown *(Diagram D)*. Keep the humps nicely rounded.

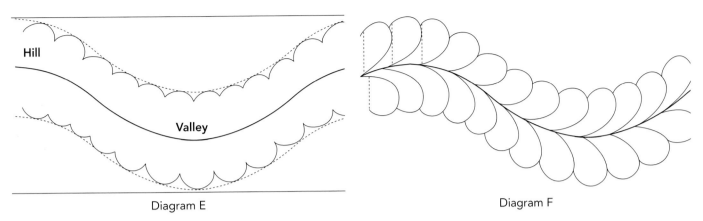

Hill

Valley

Diagram E

Diagram F

Curving Feathers On another piece of paper, draw a curving center vein line as shown in *Diagram E*. By eye, draw outer guidelines 1" to each side of this curved line. Use a penny to draw helping scallops just inside the outer guidelines on each side. Make sure you draw almost a half circle, not just a short arc, each time you use the penny. Complete the half hearts as shown in *Diagram F*. As you draw, be sure the tail of each heart is directly opposite the beginning of the scallop. As you feather your way along these "hills" and "valleys," the half heart tips back and forth. On the "hills" you will have plenty of room for the top humps of the hearts and the bottom tails. In the "valleys," you will have more space between one tail and the next. The smoother your center vein, the more naturally your heart tails will flow into it.

Feather Circles Begin by drawing a circle the outer dimension you desire. For example, if you want an 11" circle to fill a 12" setting block, first draw an 11" circle. Draw another circle within the first one for your center vein. Finally, draw a smaller circle inside the second one. The final circle is the guideline for the inner feather ring. Choose a coin to use for your helping scallops. A nickel works well for an 11" circle. Draw helping scallops just inside the outer guidelines of both rings. Feather the circle. The outer ring of feathers is like a continuous "hill." The inner ring is like a continuous "valley." Make sure the ending tail of each half heart is directly opposite the beginning of the hump. You will have many more feathers in the outer ring than in the inner one.

Princess Feather Fold a 10" piece of tracing paper in half both ways to make center guidelines. Open out and trace the design above on one quadrant. Rotate paper to trace design in all four quadrants. This design will fit a 12" block nicely.

> Sew **Smart**™
>
> For many designs, all you need to create is one quadrant. Fold paper in fourths to form center guidelines. Create the design by tracing it in each quadrant. —Marianne